The Ultimate Law Firm Associate's *Working-from-Home* Marketing Checklist

The Renowned Step-By-Step,
Year-By-Year Process for
Lawyers Who Want to
Develop Clients

The Ultimate Law Firm Associate's Working-from-Home Marketing Checklist

The Renowned Step-By-Step, Year-By-Year Process for Lawyers Who Want to Develop Clients

by

Ross Fishman, JD
CEO, Fishman Marketing, Inc.

© 2020 by Fishman Marketing, Inc.
All rights reserved.

Published by Ross Fishman, Highland Park, Illinois
fishmanmarketing.com

ISBN: 979-8-6361045-5-1

Manufactured in the United States

Cover design by Michelle Benjamin

No part of this document may be reproduced or transmitted in any form by any means, electronic or mechanical, including photocopying, recording or by information storage and retrieval system, without permission from the publisher.

Testimonials

Testimonials

*"An **important, common-sense approach** to business development for associates at every level. Use this checklist to promote a thoughtful marketing discussion and real action."*

Eileen Cohen Billinson, Principal at Billinson Latorre
Former Director of Business Development, Morgan Lewis

*"This is **an incredibly useful resource** to get associates on track towards productive, career-long, business development habits."*

Bettina Rutherford, Business Development Manager, K&L Gates

*"I have used Ross's **highly practical framework** in several firms and **strongly recommend it.** It helps lawyers demystify marketing and business development and take concrete, manageable actions to achieve success on their own terms and according to their own style. I have seen it literally give hope to associates who thought that developing a sustaining legal practice was beyond their ability."*

Nathan Darling, Chief Marketing Officer, Beveridge and Diamond
Legal Marketing Associations (LMA) President, 2010

*"Ross's Checklist is my go-to for both casual 'stop-by' conversations with associates and formal associate-training programs. With **clear guidelines** for marketing and business development by experience level, this tool is **immensely helpful.** I've had many partners comment on how smart this checklist is, and that they wish they had something like this when they were coming up the ranks."*

Jennifer Shankleton, Director of Marketing, Brouse McDowell

"Ross's insightful checklist is a practical guide to marketing yourself at every stage of your career. His book details realistic and attainable marketing and business development activities. I am a fifth-year associate and have been implementing the recommendations for a few years and can already see how they are positioning me to generate business in the future. **I strongly recommend this valuable checklist** *to associates at all levels—from first-year lawyers fresh out of school to senior associates who are eligible for partner.*
Thank you, Ross!"

Randall Borek, Fifth-Year Associate, Murphy & Hourihane

"This book needs to be in the hands of every young associate who wants to have a successful, rewarding legal career. *Just follow this practical 'how to' guide to become a top-tier rainmaker in your firm, large or small. The practical links to cogent examples add to the effectiveness and bring it alive for the reader.*
This checklist should be a 'best seller.'"

Ron Henry, Law Firm Consultant, The Garver Group, Inc.
President, Association of Legal Administrators (ALA), 2002-03

"Ross has turned an intimidating and challenging process into simple, practical, and systematic steps. **I have used his checklist for many years with great success.** *He has removed the 'deer in the headlights' moment and crafted something associates can use to see success."*

Aleisha Gravit, Chief Marketing Officer, Akin Gump
LMA President, 2013

*"Practical and engaging, Ross's step-by-step, thoughtful and practical advice helps lawyers succeed. A valuable tool both for associates and their mentors, it **should be in the hands of every lawyer!** It takes the mystery out of developing a book of business."*

Hallie J. Mann, Executive Director, Lawyers Associated Worldwide

"Essential reading for every associate at any point in their career! *Every lawyer can use this comprehensive checklist to jumpstart, or build on, their efforts to grow their reputation and successfully achieve their professional goals. In an industry defined by how your clients and peers speak of you, this checklist holds all the secrets to creating a powerful referral network.* **It is marketing nirvana."**

Nathaniel Slavin, Principal, Wicker Park Group
LMA President, 2007

"A must-read for all associates."

Allan Slagel, Partner, Taft Stettinius & Hollister

ADDITIONAL BOOKS BY ROSS FISHMAN

WE'RE SMART. WE'RE OLD. AND WE'RE THE BEST AT EVERYTHING.

The World's First No-BS Guide to Legal Marketing and Branding.

THE ULTIMATE LAW FIRM ASSOCIATE'S MARKETING CHECKLIST (CHINESE EDITION)

Edited by Cherry Zhang, LL.M.

THE ULTIMATE WOMEN ASSOCIATES' LEGAL MARKETING CHECKLIST

With Susan Freeman, M.A.

THE ULTIMATE LAW STUDENT GET-A-JOB CHECKLIST

Edited by Kerriann Stout, Esq.

THE ULTIMATE GUIDE TO STAYING SAFE IN YOUR TEENS AND 20'S

Real-Life Rules to Surviving a Pandemic, Underage Drinking, Illegal Drugs, Talking Your Way Out of a Ticket, Painless Police Stops, Sexting, and Social Media

Available at fishmanmarketing.com and Amazon.com

Dedication

Dedication

This book is dedicated to the hard-working law firm associates who strive to master a complex and challenging craft. They work long hours for demanding clients, both inside and outside their firms. They graduated into an uncertain economy, in a profession with high billable hours but low client loyalty. Controlling their own book of business is the only professional safety net that exists.

This special 2020 "Working-From-Home" edition was developed in response to the global Coronavirus (COVID-19) pandemic that is having a devastating impact on our economy and making unprecedented changes to our lives. Across the industry, law firms have sent lawyers and administrative professionals home to telecommute, to maintain their workloads, often while entertaining or homeschooling their children. Access to office buildings are off limits, encompassing physical files, client records, pre-bills, and in-person interactions.

It is an unprecedented time to be a lawyer, or any other worker, on a massive global scale. As society at large grapples with the meanings of "shelter-in-pace" and "essential" in the context of business and social conduct, lawyers are in the unique position of both living under these guidelines and advising clients regarding how to navigate around them.

To add to the complexity, government-issued guidelines are unclear and changing rapidly. Government incentives such as the CARES Act, designed to help stabilize the economy, come with their own set of challenges as many provisions are vague, leaving lawyers to scramble to best interpret their meanings, on a real-time basis, for data-hungry clients.

The Ultimate Law Firm Associate's Working-from-Home Marketing Checklist

As mentioned, the economic implications are far ranging. Most firms aren't certain how to handle this vastly different economic situation. This is *terra incognita*; we've seen recessions before, but nothing like this. We're all working together to figure out how to deal with The New Normal, and I've invited some of the best minds in law and marketing to offer their unique insight and perspective.

We offer this Special Edition to help keep lawyers on track in their client-development activities, while many of the traditional tools, like speaking at conferences, visiting clients, and meeting in-person, are currently unavailable. Entire industries are downsizing, while small businesses are failing. Law firms have seen this movie before and are tightening their belts in anticipation—laying off personnel, renegotiating leases and other contractual obligations, and slashing charitable contributions and sponsorships. Travel is prohibited for safety and financial reasons. The economic contraction will generate less legal work, and when this all blows over, we can expect even more "right-sizing" layoffs.

Building or strengthening your marketing platform now will help prepare you for whatever comes next. It can position you as an associate the firm can't afford to lose, or ready you to hang out your own shingle as a solo practitioner if the firm can't keep you around. **Follow these steps and you'll be better able to steer your own career, regardless of what the future holds for you or the legal profession.**

We're all in this together, and together we'll come through this. But your career is in your own hands. I'd encourage you to seek to make the most of it.

Good luck and stay safe!

Ross

Table of Contents

SECTION	PAGE
Acknowledgments	19
Preface	21
Introduction	27
First-Year Associates	35
Second-Year Associates	51
Third-Year Associates	55
Fourth- and Fifth-Year Associates	67
A Plea to Focus Your Marketing	69
More Activities for Fourth- and Fifth-Year Associates	83
Sixth Plus-Year Associates	97
Social Media Tools	103
Business Cards	117
Networking and Attending Seminars	121
Conduct a "Needs Assessment"	129
General Mindset	133
Gender-Based Communication Musings	135
Your Mental Health	141
Conclusion	145
Author Biography	147
Addendum	151

©2020 Fishman Marketing, Inc. All rights reserved. Do not duplicate.

Book Overview

Marketing's not difficult. Plan, prepare, and execute steadily over time. A little bit every week. *Drip, drip, drip.* Just make sure the things you are doing are the *right* things.

That's what this book is designed to facilitate. Here's the basic overview:

- ❑ **Learn to be a competent lawyer,** emphasizing both technical skills and client service. You can't just bring in the work, you gotta be able to do it too.

- ❑ **Become the sought-after subject-matter expert on a hot new area of law,** piece of legislation, or stimulus-package provision that is complex, vague, or ever-changing.

- ❑ **Develop a narrow specialty or industry niche in an area you enjoy.** Avoid becoming one more generic generalist; seek to *dominate* something. Identify a specialized trade group to target your networking and client development. Make yourself unique and indispensable to your clients, partners, and colleagues.

- ❑ **Build your newly acquired subject-matter expertise into your long-term marketing infrastructure**—the social media platform and other tools you'll leverage through partnership and beyond. This is particularly important now, when it's difficult to meet in person.

- ❑ **Be proactive in looking for ways to promote your newfound expertise** internally and externally. Offer to draft client alerts and other legal insights that can be promoted via the firm's internal and external channels. Offer to use your subject-matter knowledge to help partners prepare content for webinars, podcasts, or other programmatic ventures.

- **Join a local bar association,** interact regularly with your peers, get active, and build your professional resume.

- **Learn how to use Zoom and nurture your existing network.** Use it as a platform to initiate and maintain contact with partners and associates you interact with regularly and update them on your subject-matter research and analysis. Ask for opportunities to create additional touches with their clients and prospects to share your knowledge.

- **Build your personal brand.** When you can't build it in person, get active on social media to spread the word. Use your subject-matter experience as a jumping off point, share firm-generated or third-party content specific to your area of expertise, including a short blurb about its relevance.

- **Look for additional cross-selling opportunities with existing clients.** If your firm has an industry-team marketing platform, be sure to attend the team conference calls or Zoom meetings and ask to get on the agenda where you can share updates on your subject-matter area with a broad group of partners and other associates who are members of that industry team.

Book Overview

- ❑ As you get more experienced, spend more time out of the office with prospects and referral sources. Until it's safe to be with them in person, do this online.

That's the big picture; the rest of the book will detail the specific activities. If you ever have any questions, contact me at ross@fishmanmarketing.com or any of the experts named in this book; we'd all be happy to help you address your individual concerns.

Acknowledgments

Acknowledgments

First, I'd like to sincerely thank the dedicated marketers identified below who contributed to this special edition—some of the best minds in legal marketing worldwide. During a time of great confusion, stress, and turmoil, they nonetheless made the effort to share their expertise, seeking to help hard-working young lawyers who suddenly found themselves with an uncertain future. And a particular shout out to **Andrew Fishman, Kathleen Flynn,** and **Lisa Vicine** for their especially significant contributions.

- **Kristyn Brophy,** Marketing Manager, Conn Kavanaugh, Boston, MA
- **Dave Bruns,** Director of Client Services, Farella Braun & Martel, San Francisco, CA
- **Antonia Burrows,** Marketing Manager, Higgs & Johnson, The Bahamas
- **Andrew Fishman,** LSW, Clinician, Jewish Children and Family Services, Chicago
- **Kathleen Flynn,** Marketing and BD Consultant, Ackert Advisory, Walnut Creek, CA
- **Sue-Ella Prodonovich,** Principal, Prodonovich Advisory, Sydney, Australia
- **Roy Sexton,** Director of Marketing, Clark Hill, Saline, MI
- **Sarah Tetlow,** Owner, Firm Focus, San Francisco, CA
- **Lisa Vicine,** Chief Marketing Officer, Arnall Golden Gregory, Atlanta, GA

Preface

Preface

The law is a challenging, competitive profession; many associates live in a constant state of unease. Throw Coronavirus (COVID-19) into the mix, and you have a perfect storm of anxiety-driven emotion that can lead to feelings of confusion, concern, and worry. Social distancing can exacerbate this with isolation, loneliness, and depression. Associates want to know how they compare to their peers in the firm, across town, and around the industry. And the anxiety doesn't go away as they advance through their careers. In fact, it often *increases*, as they wonder if there's more they could be doing to improve their chance of partnership or autonomy, including developing their own clients.

I regularly see smart, personable, highly motivated senior associates or junior partners who have been working tirelessly on client development for many years, with nothing to show for it. After we sit down and discuss their marketing efforts thus far, it's often obvious to me that the activities they'd been undertaking had little chance of success. I don't want to discourage them, even when I'd like to say, "Yeah, that stuff was never going to work." It's not their fault; they just got bad advice. Or no advice at all.

I vividly remember my years as a litigation associate, receiving at most a few hours of marketing training per year. Eventually, I left the practice of law to market law firms full time, first as a big-firm Marketing Director, then Marketing Partner. There was always a steady stream of associates dropping by my office, hungry for practical, realistic advice and assistance. The guidance they'd received from their bosses and mentors tended toward "Here's what *I* did [i.e., 30 years ago, before the Internet.]."

This continues today, with many firms wanting to conduct their marketing training using their successful rainmaking senior partners.

The logic is that they *must* know how to do it, because they have a lot of business. It makes sense in theory—but it rarely works in practice. I've participated in hundreds of law firm marketing training programs and retreats, many of which included presentations by firm rainmakers, only a handful of whom actually offered useful advice.

Candidly, most of these well-intentioned rainmakers have no idea *how* they generated the business. They might *think* they know, but it's just their gut feeling or a starry-eyed retrospective. They know *something* worked, but only rarely what it *really* was. Further, the world is so different today than it was 10, 20, or 30 years ago when a 40- or 60-year-old rainmaker was building his or her practice. Back then, it was a seller's market for legal services. There were no global firms. No legal-outsourcing companies. No Internet or social media. You could hear the clacking of the secretaries' typewriters. And no novel coronavirus.

"There's a psychology term called 'survivorship bias' which says that people who succeed often attribute their success to the wrong things. Just because you happened to live to 100 doesn't mean that it was *because* of the cigarettes you smoked every day—it was more likely in *spite* of it.

"The rainmakers probably have no actual idea why they succeeded, they just assume that they made all the right choices and are happy to recommend them to anyone who will listen, even if it's terrible advice." – Andrew Fishman

And if a rainmaker *can* comprehend and distill down all of the behaviors that led her to become successful into meaningful tips for an associate, that will not guarantee that those methods will work for any particular lawyer, who has a different skillset and life experiences. There will likely need to be some adaptation to suit the associate's goals and align with the relationships they have built with their peers, prospects, and existing clients. The challenge is that associates may have neither the insights nor the experience to identify just how and when to apply adaptive methods.

It's also hard to credibly offer networking advice to a 30-year-old lawyer when your LinkedIn profile has no text, one connection, and you don't know your password. Typical associate laments include:

- "What she *really* did was inherit a book of business from a retired partner."

- "[Joe Rainmaker] is charming, funny, and the life of the party; he's out drinking with prospects every night and has a 6 handicap. I'm introverted—his methods are never going to work for me."

- "I'm already billing 1,800 hours. I don't have time to market."

- "She keeps saying, 'Good work is the best marketing.' What, our competitors aren't good lawyers too?"

- "He says he gets clients by 'providing excellent client service,' but his dad is a U.S. Senator!"

- "He made one friend in his whole life, and *that* guy became GC of a big bank and gives him all his legal work. That's not strategy, that's dumb luck."

So, without sufficient guidance or an effective roadmap, associates' business-development activities tend toward occasional and opportunistic rather than proactive and strategic. Betting their future success on happenstance or providence won't cut it. "Hope" is not a strategy. They need a plan.

Since opening Fishman Marketing 20 years ago, I've conducted 300 firm retreats and marketing training programs. I've seen the exact same nervousness in associates at nearly every single firm, from Illinois to Istanbul. From Ghana to Gary, Indiana.

Lawyers and marketers alike kept asking for a simple, practical, and detailed guide that associates could follow—a step-by-step, year-by-year list of precisely what marketing and business development activities to undertake to help avoid inefficient floundering and increase the chance that they'll have their own business when they need it. What follows is that guide.

If you have any comments or suggestions for improvements, please feel free to email them to me at ross@fishmanmarketing.com.

Good luck!

Introduction

Introduction

As a new associate, your goal should not be to bring in work, but to master the skills you need to be an excellent lawyer and to put yourself in the best-possible position to successfully develop a pipeline of high-quality legal work *later* when you will be expected to generate work or create business opportunities.

To do that, your goal from the very beginning of your associate career should be to build a strong and productive network. Gradually and systematically, over time, you will want to build a tight 250–500-person group of people who hire lawyers, influence the hiring decisions, or refer business to them.

Few clients will hire an associate for a larger case or deal; you simply don't offer enough cover if a representation were to go bad. ("Wait, you hired an *associate* for this???") Spend these important early years building your resume, reputation, and name recognition within a significant, specific target audience.

Note: **In the longer term, the likeliest path to having a sustainable, portable practice is to become one of the go-to experts in a small niche industry or sub-subset of a larger industry**—clients declare "industry expertise" to be among the traits they value most in their lawyers. Your goal shouldn't be "more marketing" but rather to become a member of the "automatic short list" for some type of representation. This expertise may evolve over time as conditions and the economy changes.

As a junior partner, a friend of mine developed a $2 million-per-year book of sustainable business just filing "small, Midwest-based securities-industry broker-dealer raiding lawsuits." (I discuss this niche strategy in greater detail below, under "A Plea to Focus Your Marketing.")

While having characterized COVID-19 thus far as having a broad and devastating effect on a global scale, it can provide an opportunity for an associate to rise above the ranks by demonstrating an ability to become a go-to resource within the firm, and specifically for busy partners, on a critical issue that many firm clients are facing.

For example, Arnall Golden & Gregory, a 180-lawyer firm, held a webinar that broadly covered the CARES Act and also took smaller deep dives into specific areas related to tax, SBA, employment, healthcare, real estate, FDA, and compliance. Busy partners asked associates to quickly help develop webinar content, including reviewing 800 pages of the Act and distilling certain provisions down into meaningful and actionable insights for clients. The webinar received 900 registrants and 700 attendees.

All participating associates received credit during the webinar for assisting with the content and are now part of the team working to field follow-up questions from clients and prospects. These efforts provided associates with exposure to external clients and internal constituents and positioned them as subject-matter experts in specific CARES Act provisions.

When the economic conditions suggest that layoffs might be inevitable, it is essential to ensure you are seen as having technical or industry skills your firm cannot afford to lose. Do a careful self-assessment to determine whether the work you do is a commodity or vital to the firm's future. Make a business case for moving yourself to a mission-critical area.

This is an essential time to ensure that the firm's leaders see the value you provide. Although no one likes a braggart, now is not the time for false modesty.

"Consider which industries will need help when this is all over. What businesses are either growing fast or in distress? Retool your practice as necessary. Obviously, labor and employment and bankruptcy are currently in high demand. What others will need legal help? Likely areas include litigation, hospitality, airlines, insurance coverage, health care, cannabis, telecommunications, and privacy and data security." – Timothy Corcoran, Principal, Corcoran Consulting Group

As an associate, focus on helping people, not looking for legal work. You want to be viewed as a knowledgeable, trusted industry insider, not a needy salesperson. Build a large number of close relationships following the steps below and you'll significantly increase the chance that you'll have your own clients later. Dave Bruns, the Director of Client Services for Farella Braun & Martel, recommends to strategically "give to get" down the road. That is, it's not a direct quid quo pro, but strategic givers win over the long term.

In all your networking, remember, as Jeffrey Horn, Managing Director of The Business Development Group says, *"It's better to be interested than to be interesting."* Be interested in them and in facilitating their success, more than being the center of attention. Just because the stereotypic rainmakers are gregarious doesn't mean that's why they get hired. Being outgoing can make it easier for them to grow their networks. But they tend to get hired because they are good at *listening* and finding ways to help people solve their problems. *That's* the secret.

As my father used to say, "When you're talking, you're not selling." We recommended many activities in this book, but they're not intended to be all-encompassing or mandatory. You needn't follow every single step. If you don't want to give speeches, for example, if that's not your thing, that's entirely OK. Maybe do a little more of some of the other things. Just be intentional, deliberate, and consistent over time.

And if you've always been reluctant to give presentations, consider whether you might be able to add more speeches to your marketing mix now that you'll be talking to a webcam rather than a ballroom. You may find that smaller Zoom meetings might be just your thing. You don't need to present to hundreds to be successful. Large audiences help build your brand and reputation, but small, interactive groups bring in work.

And if you're in a hurry, i.e. you got a late start, that's OK, you just may need to compress the timeline. If you're starting your own practice or are at a smaller firm where you're expected to bring in clients right away, you have less time to develop your legal skills and market reputation. You'll need to get out there, meet people, leverage existing relationships, and find that critical business or industry niche that will give you something credible to sell (see the chapter entitled "A Plea to Focus Your Marketing"). It's advisable to read this entire book, so you understand the big picture, then focus on the tools appropriate for your level.

The landmark article "Herding Cats: The Lawyer Personality Revealed" by Dr. Larry Richard showed that lawyers have "an average Sociability score of only 12.8%, compared to an average of 50% for the general public." The good news is, although you might be quiet, shy, and hate marketing, most of your competitors are the same way. Here's *Ross's First Rule of Legal Marketing:* "You don't have to be great. Just don't suck as bad as your competitors."

Introduction

Marketing's not hard. It's just hard *work*.

Today's Coronavirus-weakened economy has made all the traditional client-development challenges even more difficult. Legal work is shifting. We may find that there's much less overall work, or that it's simply rapidly moving into different areas, like bankruptcy, labor & employment, and insurance recovery, for example. Many of the tools in a rainmaker's typical toolkit don't currently apply. So, it's time to develop new ones, or use the modern tools more effectively.

That's good news for younger lawyers, because they're more comfortable using many of those new tools. When you can't be face-to-face with your targets, technology must fill in the gaps. And most of the senior-partner rainmakers did not grow up with a smartphone in their pudgy little toddler hands. Most lawyers over 50 didn't touch a computer until they were already practicing law. Lawyers over 40 didn't learn computer skills until high school, and 60-year-old lawyers had to learn about the internet when they were at least 35 years old. You have a strategic advantage. This new world order fits your personal style.

Most of today's associates don't remember a time when they didn't carry a phone with them throughout the day. So, while a firm's senior partners might have a general awareness of LinkedIn, most don't know how to use it especially well. They use Facebook to connect with their grandchildren. Very few will have Twitter, Instagram, or Snapchat accounts. Most think TikTok is the sound their wind-up analog watches make.

This is your time. Your life experiences have positioned you to excel under these very circumstances. This is a devastating time for the world and the US economy. But the sliver of silver lining in this confusing mess is that chaos creates opportunity, and you can use it to significantly advance your career. You have a lifetime of valuable experience and relationships; it's time to leverage them.

Lindsay Hamilton, the CMO of Walkers in the Cayman Islands, suggests that "Client care, service, and relevance are the lens for business development during tumultuous times. Maintain a client-first mindset. This includes being hyper-relevant—help your clients cut through the noise on what impacts they may face and potential solutions that may be applicable to their business."

When economic conditions suggest that layoffs might be inevitable, it is essential to ensure you have skills your firm cannot afford to lose. Do a careful self-assessment to determine whether the work you do is a commodity or important to the firm's future. Make a case for moving yourself to a mission-critical area.

Ensure that the firm's leaders see the value you provide and your importance to the firm's future. Although no one likes a braggart, now is not the time for false modesty.

First-Year Associates

MINDSET:

Become an excellent lawyer.

Your first priority is to learn to be a competent lawyer; external marketing isn't important yet. Your only real proactive activity should be ensuring that you don't lose touch with the people you already know. Maintain relationships with friends from college and law school and any organizations you belong to. Implement a client-tracking system now, while your list is still manageable.

By organizing your contact list and building in personal details, such as their favorite movie, their spouse's name, and anniversary, you'll succeed in periodic outreach. Tracking personal details will help you know what to write when you conduct the outreach. You're able to inquire about the marathon they ran or congratulate them on their new baby. Create a reminder to ensure that you've had some contact with your chums once per quarter. Your future self will thank you.

For junior associates, the "clients" they need to build relationships with may be their firm's senior associates and partners.

Under normal circumstances setting up a quick Zoom, Skype, or FaceTime call with someone might seem odd. Today, under the self-isolation protocols, it's become socially acceptable and you can see many more people per week via a friendly 15-minute catch-up Skype call than when you're meeting face-to-face, which tends to be a one-hour minimum.

- ❏ This is the year you should create the basic platform you'll be working from over the next few years, the infrastructure you'll gradually expand over time.
    - ○ Join one local, state, or national bar association and get actively involved in one targeted educational committee

within your practice area. Get the benefit of all of the online content, programs, and virtual networking they're starting to offer.
- Engage with your peers. Form relationships online and meet them physically later.
- Learn your craft.
- Invest in your profession.
- Your long-term goal should be to chair a small committee during your fifth year of practice.

- [ ] Read your firm's website, internal website portal, newsletters, LinkedIn or Facebook pages, and other marketing materials to learn about its range of services and clients. You may have more downtime now, so make good use of it, or take advantage of the time you would otherwise have spent commuting.
  - Visit your firm's Coronavirus (COVID-19) webpage or collection of content on the topic. Identify where your firm may be sending redundant messages or worse, none at all. Offer to fill the gaps by developing content or organizing existing content into a logical order for client ease in navigating.
  - Read your senior associates' and partners' biographies and profiles as well, to learn about their practices and outside interests. This will come in handy later.
  - "While this project is certainly an important part of your marketing and growth, it will never occur if you are waiting to "find the time" to do it. This is why it is imperative to schedule or block off small chunks of time to devote to the project. Instead of 'review the firm's website' as a To Do, try breaking it up into a 25-minute project. You'll find that you were able to discover a lot of information about

your firm and its practice in that short amount of time." — <u>Sarah Tetlow,</u> Legal Productivity Coach, Firm Focus
  - "Educate yourself on the technology that can help, such as the Client-Relationship Management (CRM) system and Competitive Intelligence (CI) tools." Roberta Montafia, Principal, Roberta Montafia Consulting

- Build your personal brand within your law firm. Focus on internal marketing by developing relationships with your firm's lawyers, both inside and outside of your practice area.
  - Also focus on getting to know the professional staff at your firm; they will be able to serve as a sounding board and guide to internal relationships.

- If you're comfortable with new technology, take the time to learn the nuances of both Zoom and GoToMeeting. You can add value, particularly in smaller firms, by having useful technical expertise.

- Marketers often advise lawyers to avoid spending their careers eating lunch at their desk. Consider inviting colleagues to join you regularly for a virtual lunch or happy hour.
  - Invite the firm's marketer assigned to your practice area to a virtual lunch or coffee to brainstorm activities you can do *now*. They can identify for you any content or other programs in the works that you may be able to help develop or contribute to.

- Generally, seek to go out:
  - Once each week with a firm lawyer *inside* your practice area

- Twice each month with a firm lawyer *outside* of your practice area
- Regularly with friends and contacts

☐ While "sheltering in place," it is essential to maintain regular contact with people. It is easy for lawyers working at home to become reclusive. Get people on your calendar regularly for calls or teleconferences. "Out of sight, out of mind" can be dangerous to an associate's career, and emails and texts do not form the meaningful relationships you need to advance your career. You'll want to increase the number of contacts to roughly:
  - 2-3 times each week with a firm lawyer inside your practice area
  - Once a week with a firm lawyer outside of your practice area
  - Daily with friends and contacts
  - Consider hosting a cocktail hour or game night with college friends; it's a great way to stay connected and minimize the feelings of isolation.

☐ Draft a detailed **website biography,** following the firm's format.
  - Update it regularly, especially when your practice is developing.
  - Ideally you should update it every time a matter you are involved with concludes, you publish an article or give a presentation, are appointed to a committee, etc. Reach out to your marketing department to ensure these activities are tagged to your website bio.
  - Don't reinvent the wheel. Keep a simple but effective checklist of what you should update whenever you have

completed a "bio-worthy" event. Have you updated your personal resume, the firm's biography, and your LinkedIn profile? Do you have a personal blog or email newsletter that you can share with the news? Work with your marketing team to help.
- Make it a habit that when you update your biography you also update the matters you have worked on in your firm's experience- or knowledge-management system, such as Foundation. Remember to include the activities you'll be undertaking online as well.
- Update it thoroughly at least every six months.
- Be judicious in what you include. Delete all items from high school.
- Be sensible regarding college activities.

☐ Build your network. **Create a mailing list** of friends and contacts, don't forget to leverage your firm's Client Relationship Management (CRM) system, you never know where your classmates will end up. By participating in your firm's CRM program, you can leverage your relationship to help create introductions with various technology tools your firm may use, such as RelSci.

☐ Opt for more, rather than fewer people, when deciding whom to add. Now is the time to reach out authentically to contacts, schoolmates, etc. via Zoom or telephone (best and most personal), email, text, or social media. Don't forget to briefly track conversation snippets that will help you succeed in future outreach.
- Law school classmates
- Childhood, high school, and college friends
- Former colleagues

- Community association and professional club contacts
- Parents of your children's friends and contacts through your children's activities
- Your neighbors

☐ Studies vary but note that it takes at least 8 to 10 touches to get, and stay, on someone's radar. So, you need to cut through the clutter, and find comfortable and non-intrusive ways to stay in touch regularly.

☐ Keep in touch with your existing network, leveraging the full range of online tools, like:
  - Virtual events, webinars, and teleconferences.
    - Ensure you have a good-quality webcam or camera. The one on your laptop or smartphone is sufficient for these purposes. No one expects cinema quality, but you should know how to use the software.
    - Get a stick-on lens cover for your computer's webcam, so you can slide it over the lens when you're not using the camera. Just in case.
  - Add frequent virtual breakfasts, lunches, coffee, and/or drinks to your schedule. When working from home it can be too easy for lawyers to become happily reclusive. Most lawyers are introverts, so we must make an extra effort to put ourselves out there
  - Written material can be helpful, but it must be useful. Marketers today are pushing out a lot more content than usual and recipients can quickly reach the point of saturation. Provide a unique angle or perspective, don't just circulate new changes to the law or economy. Discuss its particular relevance to your clients and prospects. *That* is the value that you can provide over the generic

newsletters or alerts they might receive from a lawyer at a firm who doesn't know them intimately like you do.
- Use social media like LinkedIn, Facebook, Twitter, and Snapchat to foster engagement with your contacts.
  - It's not likely that you will have the time or persistence over the long term to be effective on all of them. So, select the one(s) you're most comfortable with and stick with them.
- If you have written or co-authored a client alert for your firm, ask Marketing to let you know when it has been posted to the firm's LinkedIn page so that you can share it directly with your Connections; make sure to do so in a timely manner.
- Read a good networking book, like the popular *Never Eat Alone* by Keith Ferrazzi.

❏ Before you engage in any marketing or social media, review
- Your firm's social media policy, including any 2020 updates
- Your state's ethics rules governing the use of marketing, communication, and social media (generally Rules 7.1–7.4; see *goo.gl/JOhhF*)

❏ **LinkedIn** will be your most-important social media platform. Lawyer biographies are no longer formal CV's; you can use LinkedIn to track your every action and article, making it more robust and insightful than your firm bio will ever be.
- If you don't have a LinkedIn profile already, create one; your marketing team can help.
- If you *do* have a LinkedIn page from college or law school, do a careful audit to ensure it is now professional. Take this opportunity to update it thoroughly.

- Sanitize it so there's nothing a 65-year-old client or the most conservative senior partner would find offensive.
- Don't identify yourself as "Attorney at XYZ Firm" in the heading space. Consider this your headline—intrigue your visitors with something differentiating.
  - Infuse it with your personality.
- Add a quality photo. No cropped vacation, group, party, or wedding pictures.
- Write in the first person with a friendly, professional tone.
- Create a custom public profile URL.
  - Learn how by going to t.ly/5PIGE
- No one expects it to be very long; you've only been a lawyer for a short while.
- Review the privacy settings.
- Generally, check it weekly. While working from home, check it more frequently than usual.
- Post occasional relevant updates, including thought-leadership pieces you have written.
- It's easy to start by sharing or liking things that others in your firm or professional network have posted.
- Remember, listening and engaging with what others post is as important in social networking as what you say and post.
- Join your law school LinkedIn alumni group and your firm's LinkedIn group.
- Build your LinkedIn network; connect with friends, peers, co-workers, acquaintances, classmates, referral sources, and clients.
- Consider starting a group for your law school graduating class.
- Regularly "Endorse" clients, friends, peers, co-workers, prospects, and referral sources; it only takes a click. They'll typically endorse you back.

- A word of caution with Skills + Endorsements: When you receive an endorsement from someone for a specific skill, only post it on your bio if you have actual expertise in that area. Some state bar rules have restrictions on this.
- When in doubt, leave it off.
- Read "How to Draft a Persuasive LinkedIn Profile" in the Addendum.
- DO NOT be afraid to ask your marketing team for help with profile optimization, content sharing and building connections. You would be surprised how much you can learn with a social media/LinkedIn savvy marketer in just 15 minutes.
- "While scrolling through LinkedIn, you will frequently see a milestone that someone in your network has achieved. A birthday, a work anniversary, or a new job. Before you select the auto-populated "Congrats!" "Nice work!" "Wow, already?!", stop and ask yourself if mailing a short, handwritten card is appropriate. Usually it is and you will stand out from everyone else by going the extra mile...or the extra stamp." — Sarah Tetlow

❏ Consider asking your Marketing professionals to purchase ClearView Social, a tool which can magnify the impact of the firm's thought leadership by simplifying the scheduling and repetition of sharing across the various platforms, e.g. LinkedIn, Twitter, etc., and providing helpful analytics. See clearviewsocial.com

❏ If you don't have a **Facebook** page already, create one.
  - If you do have a Facebook page from college or law school, do a thorough audit to ensure it is now professional.
  - Update your security settings.

- Hide the party photos.
- Sanitize it so there's nothing a 65-year-old client or the most-conservative senior partner would find offensive.
- Keep it casual and sensible.
- Check it at least weekly.
- Join your law school alumni Facebook group.
- Connect with your friends, especially those from law school.

☐ If you don't have a **Twitter** account, create one under your name.

☐ "Make sure to keep your private Twitter account separate from your professional Twitter account. You will not want your professional Twitter account to reflect any of your personal opinions, perspectives, or preferences that could alienate or offend existing and potential clients. Keep your professional Twitter posts just that … professional." — Lisa Vicine, CMO, Arnall Golden & Gregory
  - Other marketers recommend using just one Twitter account for both personal and professional purposes, to create a single unified online persona. This would mean tempering your personal posts to ensure they are always appropriate for your professional audience as well.

☐ If you enjoy using Twitter as a social media platform:
  - Check it occasionally.
  - Build your Twitter network; connect with contacts, clients, and thought leaders.
  - Post at least weekly on something relating to your job or interests.
  - Retweet tweets that resonate with you.

- Consider utilizing Twitter as a *listening* platform to better understand clients, prospects, competitors, scholars, and more.
- Pay attention to what they are promoting, discussing, or commenting on. It can all be valuable.
- Follow people, companies, associations, and organizations within your legal, business, and general areas of interest.

❏ Sign up for **Google Alerts** at *google.com/alerts* or Mention at mention.com/en. See video at *goo.gl/bAeQhj*
  - For the Search Terms, use "[your name]" and "[your firm's name]" (in quotes).
  - Consider also creating alerts on friends, relatives, and prospects.
  - Drop them a quick email when you see them mentioned.
  - Even more powerful is a short, handwritten note. Weigh the speed of a response via email, text, Slack, Facebook, etc. with the visceral impact of a handwritten letter.
  - Reach out to your firm's librarian or other information-systems professional to identify other alerts and news feeds you may want to subscribe to. If your firm does not have one, contact your local public or law library and enlist the assistance of the research librarians. They can be a valuable asset.

❏ Develop a reputation for providing the highest-quality **client service**.
  - Remember, the profession is full of smart, technically skilled lawyers.
    - Clients truly value lawyers who excel at communication, timeliness, and accessibility.

- Keep clients regularly informed regarding the current status of their matters.
  - Send them copies of all relevant correspondence.
- *Always* call clients back promptly, ideally within two hours. Better, ask each client how soon they like their calls returned and meet their preferred schedule. There's no one-size-fits-all solution to client service.
  - Consider: if you have a sick child, how would you feel about a pediatrician who has an "All calls returned within 24 hours" policy?
- Have a system in place that ensures that *someone* responds promptly when you are unavailable. For example, some lawyers have their assistants check their phone messages regularly.
  - Have him/her return the client's call.
  - Explain that you will be unavailable until a particular time. Ask if they would like their call returned then, or if they would prefer having someone else address the issue sooner.
- Give clients and prospects your cell phone number.
  - They will appreciate the offer and won't abuse the privilege with late night or weekend calls.
  - Consumer clients (e.g. divorce and criminal defense) are the exception. They *will* call, so be cautious.
- "A good question to ask all clients at the beginning of a relationship is "What do you consider 'end of day'? 5:00 pm EST, 5:00 pm PST, midnight? It can change for every person which could be a deal breaker if you are tardy with work product, or force someone to work into the evening when they had expected to receive the document from you earlier." – Dave Bruns

- Instead of simply *meeting* your client deadlines, try to *beat* them by at least a day or two. Don't leave clients sweating about whether their critical document will arrive on time. They'll feel much better without the added stress. Simply docket the deadline earlier and work toward the artificial date instead.
    - This works for your internal audience as well. Strive to consistently beat the work deadline, giving the senior associate or partner more time to review or work on it. They'll look favorably on this.
- Check your email at least once every night and daily on weekends. As important as it is to be extremely responsive, it's also important to maintain down time. As such, be deliberate as to when you are checking your emails in the evenings and on weekends. Turn off sound and notifications and *choose* when it is a convenient time to check in briefly.
- "Be mindful of when you send emails during off hours to partners, colleagues and clients. A response at 2:00 am that disturbs someone's sleep may not be viewed in the best light, contrary to your view it will be seen that you are working at all hours. If you happen to draft a late-night response, schedule it to send at a reasonable hour the next morning." — Lisa Vicine
    - Learn to use the "Delay or schedule sending email messages" feature in Outlook. See t.ly/G2XdE
- When telecommuting, you may quickly start to feel like you are *always* at work.

❑ If you're starting your own firm,
- Find a way to connect with a senior lawyer—a mentor who can offer guidance, help teach you some skills, and throw you some overflow work.

The Ultimate Law Firm Associate's Working-from-Home Marketing Checklist

- - You can reciprocate by helping with their basic social media or technology.
- Your initial clients will likely be your historic relationships.
- You can find many practical new resources dedicated to this area online. Also:
  - Consider joining the American Bar Association's GPSolo group, at *americanbar.org/groups/gpsolo/*
  - Buy Jay Foonberg's best-selling *"How to Start and Build a Law Practice"* book at *t.ly/MgzN9*

Second-Year Associates

MINDSET:

Build your internal brand and develop your network.

Second-Year Associates

Your first priority as a second-year associate remains learning to be a great lawyer; marketing is still a distant second. Continue to focus on building your internal brand for excellence, efficiency, and teamwork.

- ❑ Stay in touch with your friends and contacts.
   - Leverage Zoom, GoToMeeting, FaceTime, Skype, and other technology to connect with at least a few people every day, just to say a quick hello and stay on their radar screen. The telephone works just fine for quick "touching base" calls.
   - Don't assume that all of your clients want to use new videoconferencing technology. Our job is to make them comfortable, so ask each client what works best for *them*. They may have a weak home WiFi signal, or messy hair and no make-up. Some, particularly older or more formal people, might prefer the telephone.

- ❑ Continue the "First-Year Associates" activities, above.

- ❑ Continue adding new names to your mailing list and to your LinkedIn and Facebook networks as you encounter these contacts. If you have not already started a personal client tracker, begin preparing one now with pertinent contact information, last date connected, and some personalized notes.
   - Bar association committee members
   - Your peers within client companies
   - People you meet at networking functions
   - Alumni association contacts
   - Co-counsel and opposing counsel
   - Referral sources with mutual client targets including strategic advisors, accounting firms, and financial advisors

The Ultimate Law Firm Associate's Working-from-Home Marketing Checklist

- ❏ Don't forget to include them in the firm's mailing list as well. Remember, you need to create regular, consistent contacts to get and stay "top of mind." The content your firm creates and distributes can help with this.

- ❏ Join LinkedIn groups of the associations and industries you are involved in.
  - Pay attention to the conversations.
  - Learn who are the industry leaders and influencers.

- ❏ Read legal profession trade magazines, law-specific blogs, and online news sources to improve your technical skills.
  - Link to articles that demonstrate your professional interests or expertise
  - Work with your library or information-services professionals to get daily news feeds

- ❏ Volunteer for firm committees and activities. It's a great way to raise your profile and get to know people in other areas of the firm.
  - "Offer to help with firm activities, e.g. rebuilding together, participating in food bank drives, etc. Be an active member of the firm 'family.'" — Dave Bruns
  - Help with practice group activities such as drafting matters for rankings and awards like *Chambers* directories.
  - Help firm lawyers or business-development professionals compile client pitches and presentations, to gain an understanding of the process.

Third-Year Associates

MINDSET:

Continue developing your external network, including relationships with your in-house contemporaries.

Start developing a toolkit of the soft skills that will become increasingly important to your success, e.g., an elevator speech, public speaking, writing or co-authoring articles or blog posts, and interpersonal communication skills to inspire confidence.

By now you're getting a better handle on your legal practice. Continue improving your technical skills, but you can begin to be more proactive in growing your network.

- ❏ Continue the First- and Second-Year Associates activities, above.

- ❏ Build your resume by participating more actively in your bar association within your practice area.
    - ○ Volunteer for a committee and work toward a leadership position.
    - ○ Write a brief article for a committee newsletter.
    - ○ Give a speech on an area of particular interest.
    - ○ Consider hosting a webinar that you can jointly present with a colleague.

- ❏ "Increase your marketing efforts; devote time each week to a proactive networking activity, e.g., meals, sports, music, professional events, etc. When under a 'social distancing' protocol, simply make them virtual, including e.g. hosting a virtual coffee hour, happy hour, book club, lunch or, as one lawyer recently did, a Zoom scotch tasting with law school colleagues!" — Kathleen Flynn, Ackert Advisory
    - ○ Create a plan to regularly connect with your list of top prospects and referral sources.
    - ○ Come prepared to ask well-informed questions about their business and their current struggles.
    - ○ Don't forget to leverage your firm's competitive-intelligence and knowledge-management tools. Remember that "it's more important to be interested than interesting."
    - ○ Listen for opportunities to help them achieve their goals.
    - ○ Find ways to help them become successful in their careers

- Nancy Myrland, President of Myrland Marketing, suggests asking questions like:
  - How are things going at your company?
  - What kind of issues are you dealing with right now?
  - What are the most pressing issues that you have to solve?
  - What has surprised you the most?
  - How are you doing personally with all of this?
  - Are you working from home?
  - How is that going?
  - If your company hasn't sent everyone home to work yet, how does that make you feel? I would imagine it would be a little frightening right about now.
  - Is there anything at all I can do to help?

☐ Master a basic **"elevator speech"** (how-to information is available online). This is a good time to practice with those you are sheltering in place with. You have a captive audience!
- Tell people what you do in a memorable, personal way.
  - Avoid using jargon.
  - Talk about the *benefits* of what you do.
  - Keep it so simple that a child could understand it.
  - Watch the video at *t.ly/pZxGk*
- Dave Bruns reminds us that "the goal is to get them interested in speaking with you, not shut down the conversation. You want them intrigued enough to ask follow-up questions, while you quickly transition the conversation back to them. It's simply a door opener—make it interesting, humorous, or personal, not technical or difficult to understand."

- ❏ Write multiple versions of your elevator pitch.
  - ○ **Quick version:** One or two sentences that describe what you do and why.
  - ○ **Medium version:** One to two paragraphs; an expansion of your quick version of the what and the why to include the who.
  - ○ **Long version:** An expansion of your medium version; can include example clients, representative engagements, and other relevant information.
  - ○ **Alternative versions:** Create customized versions of your elevator pitch for different audiences.
  - ○ **Most importantly, a "canned" pitch isn't likely to be helpful.** The goal is to ask the other person about themselves *first*. This way, when they then ask what *you* do, you will have the information that helps you describe yourself and your practice in an advantageous way, showing them that you are knowledgeable about their business and industry.
    - Why waste time talking about things you do that they don't care about?

- ❏ In addition to your elevator pitch, have short answers ready to everyday questions such as "How are you?" Instead of saying "busy" or "swamped," have an anecdote ready about a new matter you are working on or an interesting industry-specific webinar you attended. Always remain upbeat, especially in these turbulent times.
  - ○ "Be a real person having a real conversation, even if it means admitting that you don't have all the answers but are working hard to find them, particularly in the rapidly changing COVID-19 environment." — Lisa Vicine

The Ultimate Law Firm Associate's Working-from-Home Marketing Checklist

- ○ "Consume lots of data to remain relevant. Read or scan *People* magazine when you're at the grocery store, so you are never left out of a pop-culture conversation." — Dave Bruns

- ❏ Learn to turn social contacts into potential business contacts.
  - ○ This is a long-term process; it typically takes at least 7 to 20 touch points with a new contact before you begin to have a chance of getting hired. This statistic may change under this strange new environment.
  - ○ Kathleen Flynn suggests: "Now is an excellent time to reach out to people authentically to see how they are coping with the situation. Also, have something of value you might offer to your contact--a CLE online, an insight about how this might affect their business, or even an ear or helping hand to network if they find themselves seeking new employment opportunities.
    - There may even be personal ways you can provide assistance. Did you find a great online resource for something they may need, perhaps a learning site your kids at home are using while stranded without school? Would they like to join a virtual happy hour, yoga class, etc.?

- ❏ Ask your Marketing Partner or professional to bring in networking training. Also check your local bar association for marketing gatherings via Zoom or other video conferencing platforms. Consultants and associations have already adapted to offer these training and CLE programs online.
  - ○ See the brief video at *goo.gl/Bwq9ii*
    - Networking is a learned skill. It's not difficult, but many behaviors are counterintuitive to most lawyers.
    - Most importantly, remember that work is brought in by listening, not talking.

- ❏ "Attend marketing training offered by the firm. Your marketing team may have some 'canned' training that you can take advantage of, watch video, read legal marketing blogs, etc. Now is a good time to brush up on the skills you'll need now and when things return to normal." — Kathleen Flynn
  - If the firm doesn't offer it, request it.
  - The leading firms are spending more time and effort on business-development/sales activities.
  - See the video at *goo.gl/4RxHNp*

- ❏ Look for opportunities to develop new business from existing clients (making sure to connect with the responsible partner before you engage in any client discussions).
  - Now is a critical time to be in touch with your clients. Use this time to identify areas where you can provide assistance, and not always billable work.
    - "Call and ask about how they are handling certain issues, have a discussion, brainstorm ideas, be a trusted advisor." — Kathleen Flynn
    - Find a way to work through their problems with them. Start with free advice. If it grows into a larger or more complex issue, at some point you may want to let them know that you'll need to start charging them to help them work through this issue in greater detail.
    - "Be sensitive to anything that might come across as a hard sell. People are looking for compassion and empathy. Those lawyers who provide it will be remembered. Connect with empathy first to avoid sounding tone deaf. This problem could take years to overcome." — Dave Bruns

The Ultimate Law Firm Associate's Working-from-Home Marketing Checklist

- ○ When chatting with your peers inside client companies, listen for new areas where they might need a lawyer.
  - Did they mention that they will need to downsize their salesforce? They might need an employment lawyer.
  - Did they mention that they were considering purchasing new technology or systems, buying back their stock, or suing a defaulting vendor or customer? Mention these issues to the partner in charge of the client relationship.
- ○ Sign-offs like "Let me know if I can ever be of service" are not helpful. Even though you truly mean it, they won't call; it sounds insincere and meaningless. It's our job to ask the questions that *help* them identify their actual needs.
  - Every communication should include an invitation to have a conversation. Seek to change it to a one-on-one interaction.
  - David Ackert of Ackert Advisory suggests something like "I was just thinking about you and your team. How are you holding up during this uncertain time? Let's schedule a quick call to touch base."
  - Or possibly "I've been keeping an eye on developments concerning [XYZ]. Let's get on a quick call today to discuss the potential implications to your business."
  - Or "We're starting to hear some rumblings about [XYZ]. Why don't we connect tomorrow about this for five minutes?"
  - Or "The coronavirus situation is changing rapidly. I'd like to schedule a weekly 10-min call (no charge) to keep you abreast of our recommendations."

- Jeffrey Cunix, COO and President, CACF, Inc., suggests "Call all of your clients and hot prospects simply to check in and ensure they and their families are healthy.
  - "Be a friend! Have a casual conversation and don't pitch any legal work.
  - "If they bring up a subject pertaining to business, then feel free to run with it. Otherwise, this is a caring, friendly check-in."
- Follow your target clients' competitors to develop industry intelligence and ask your peers thought-provoking questions about what their competitors are doing to gain insight into undiscovered needs.

❑ Regularly read legal and targeted industry publications, print and online.
  - Subscribe to blogs and follow Twitter accounts of leaders in these industries.
  - "Ask your partners and clients what they read. You want to read the same publications, so you can understand their perspective and develop more empathy." — Dave Bruns

❑ "Consider your competition. Many will retreat and wait for the disruption to blow over. Others will strain their relationships with inappropriately aggressive pitches. Clients will remember those who took a compassionate, client-centric approach during this time." — David Ackert

❑ Add select client and prospect names to your Google Alerts (e.g., "XYZ Company")
  - Use information you receive as a reason to contact, congratulate, or reconnect. This gives you another authentic reason to be in touch. Similar to the LinkedIn

outreach advice above, ask yourself if the news is worth a handwritten note dropped in the mail.

- ❏ "Reach out to new lateral attorneys who join your firm." — Kathleen Flynn
  - It's unlikely that you're hiring many new laterals at the moment but take this opportunity to reach out to those who might have joined pre-pandemic.
  - Introduce yourself.
  - Develop relationships and become a helpful resource.
  - They will surely appreciate the outreach at a time when they may be feeling even more disconnected, and these "touches" are not forgotten.
  - You might even learn about how you can co-market, co-serve a client, or share introductions to your respective networks.

- ❏ Get to know your firm's marketing and business-development professionals.
  - They are a great resource for you.
  - "Marketing and BD professionals are the strings that weave the firms' practices together. They know who is pitching whom, who is speaking on or specializing in certain practices or industries. They can insert you into the fabric of the firms." — Dave Bruns.
  - They often have valuable marketing opportunities to share. If they see that you respect them as professionals and value their advice and contributions, they're more likely to offer you the strategic perks that come across their desks.

- ❏ "If you are uncomfortable with the recommended marketing tools, e.g. presenting, writing a memorable LinkedIn profile,

or in using a particular technology, ask your marketers for help.
- "If your firm does not offer the assistance you need then open your own wallet and *invest in yourself.* There are many talented professional coaches out there who can help you gain the confidence you need to present virtually and use PR and social media tools effectively.
- "Still need help? Look to business associations that are geared to the legal industry such as the Legal Marketing Association (LMA), the Association of Legal Administrators (ALA), International Legal Technology Association (ILTA), and American Association of Law Libraries (AALL), as well as, the business sections of your local, state and national bar association. They all have resources available for our business development." — Roberta Montafia

❑ Update your LinkedIn profile.
- Add organizations, volunteering experience, and honors and awards.
- Add your top thought-leadership pieces to the Publications section and include a summary and the article URL.
- Consider adding most of the people you encounter in your professional life.
  - "Always include a personal note reminding new contacts how you know each other and wishing them well in an individual way. If they accept the invitation, follow up with a short note to suggest a phone call. Check out if they belong to any online groups that would be beneficial to join. Watch their posts and 'like' or comment as appropriate to signal you are engaged and care what they have to say.

The Ultimate Law Firm Associate's Working-from-Home Marketing Checklist

- "You can share your own stories and respond to other people's posts, but the real magic is in the one-to-one conversations, even when in the public or semi-public sphere. As always, you should be authentic and thoughtful. Remember, just because you are still in your yoga pants, your posts should continue to be appropriate to your network, company and profession." — <u>Lydia Bednerik Neal</u>, Blattel Communications
    - First read the "Drafting a Persuasive LinkedIn Profile" in the Addendum.

Fourth- and Fifth-Year Associates

MINDSET:

Continue refining your legal skills.

Expand your network and build your external reputation and résumé.

Focus on client-service skills and interacting with clients.

Big-firm associates may transition to Senior Associate status.

Solos and small firm associates should be gaining traction.

Remember that providing the highest-quality technical skills and extremely responsive client service are essential elements of your firm's marketing to its existing clients.

As a fifth-year lawyer, you should chair a local bar association committee as a persuasive résumé builder. You may also seek to create a new committee, to leapfrog the competition. As an example, finding that I enjoyed marketing, I contacted the American Bar Association, seeking to join the Marketing Legal Services Committee. They informed me that this group was defunct. I told them that I'd resurrect it if they'd appoint me the committee's chairman, and they agreed. I invited my boss and a couple friends and immediately grew the membership by 400%. It looked great on my nascent Marketing résumé.)

A Plea to Focus Your Marketing

A Plea to Focus Your Marketing

This is the time to start focusing your efforts more narrowly, particularly toward an industry group or subspecialty practice niche. See the videos at *goo.gl/fKR7AA* and *goo.gl/ QtmJTT*

Here's the larger point: When the next recession hits, I wouldn't want to be just another smart and skilled but generic and easily replaced generalist. I'd rather be the one who offers more, a skill or expertise that your firm can't find equally in every other associate in your class.

You also become much easier for others to cross-sell if you have a unique expertise that the partners can remember when in conversations with prospects.

> *"You manufacture bicycles? [Or build prisons, or license offshore oil-rig technology, or understand the CARES Act, or...?] One of our corporate associates has expertise in that area!"*

For new grads who are starting their own practice, it'll be a while before clients will be hiring you purely for your legal talent. But if you're the lawyer who knows their industry best, you'll have an advantage over those who may have superior legal skills but don't offer your industry insight. The fastest way for a newer lawyer to gain client-development traction is to find that specialty niche. Use these unique attributes of your life to your advantage.

For example, I probably know more about Industrial Tire Manufacturing than just about any lawyer in the world—it's my family business. My father and grandfather designed and built

The Ultimate Law Firm Associate's Working-from-Home Marketing Checklist

tires for heavy equipment, like underground mining crawlers, loaders, etc.

Growing up, the specs of new tire sizes and the composition of tire fill was typical dinner conversation. As a child, I played with toy Caterpillar forklifts. I vulcanized rubber for my fifth-grade science-fair project. I worked in the factory in high school. I've flown in the Goodyear blimp.

That is to say, I take for granted an insider's nuanced understanding of this narrow little industry. But practicing as a litigation associate, it never occurred to me that some group of companies would have found that unique insight to be valuable. Instead of marketing "general commercial litigation to Chicago-area businesses," I should have been marketing my tire-industry expertise to companies like Goodyear, John Deere, Caterpillar, the rubber importers, chemical manufacturers, and other satellite industries that support or relate to it.

They would have valued having a lawyer who knew their industry as well as they did. But it simply never occurred to me that I possessed any uniquely useful information. Now I know better.

It's not enough to specialize in the obvious industry sectors like real estate, health care, construction, financial services, or insurance—they are simply too broad. You must be more precise and find a niche within them (e.g., FCA litigator in health care, D&O liability in insurance). You will also find opportunities in smaller, more defined and obscure areas where you have existing experience, interest, or contacts. Think in terms of focusing on Pest Control rather than on Banking. Not Transportation Law but

Transportation of Infectious Biological Material. See the video at: *goo.gl/3GWNQa*

Consider segmenting it further by geography and/or the particular type of company or size of matter. The answer might not be obvious now; just look for it and recognize it when it comes along. It takes at least a few years to build this, so start being proactive in this regard beginning around your fourth year.

For example, at Fishman Marketing we have developed marketing initiatives supporting lawyers and firms who targeted niche industries or practices including these:
- *Ad valorem* property tax cases in Chicago
- Alabama pest-control companies
- Backyard barbecue propane tank explosions in Colorado
- Boy Scout abuse personal injury cases in Chicago
- Bridge-and-tunnel construction companies in Florida
- College-athletics coaches in the SEC
- Cuban personal injury cases in South Florida
- Defending the Chicago police in Taser-related cases
- Divorce cases for Iranian immigrants living in Canada
- Estate litigation in Vancouver
- Ghanaian law firm seeking inbound referrals
- Global aircraft and railcar finance under U.S. law
- Health care lobbying and intellectual property
- Health care software licensing contracts
- Multi-generational family businesses
- New York companies doing business in Israel
- Northern California agriculture industry
- Oil and gas companies in Louisiana
- Personal injury appeals
- Personal injury cases for St. Louis Catholics

- Surfing lawyer in Southern California
- Trucker DUI defense in northern British Columbia
- Upstate New York forestry and timber regulatory

Examples of the marketing materials we designed for some of them are included below.

Some creative recent examples we've seen have included firms that have developed "Coronavirus Task Forces," and practices targeting the cannabis and ride-share industries, and hair-transplant malpractice.

Considerations in identifying the niche or industry to target include:
- Did you grow up in a family business?
- What was your college major?
- What hobby, passion, or special skill or interest of yours would clients value?
- What job did you have before law school?
- What's hanging on your walls or sitting on your credenza?
- Where do you or your spouse have an established network?
- What do you know that other lawyers don't that would benefit some category of clients?
- What type of law do you practice?
- What are you seeing as growth trends within your practice?
- Think through your list of friends and family members. Are several of them in one particular industry or niche?

What market are you in and how can you leverage it? For example, Atlanta has become the world's #1 filming location. If you're a contract lawyer, consider targeting production companies, talent agencies, prop shops and others serving the industry.

Fill out one of the handy "Niche and Industry Marketing Checklists" in the Addendum.

To help you identify your narrow niche, visit a public or law library to review a printed copy of Gale Publishing's multi-volume *Encyclopedia of Associations.* It is also available with a Lexis/Nexis subscription.

- ❑ Browse through the easy-to-use 135,000-association directory to identify the best trade groups or professional associations serving your target industry.
    - ○ Seek a 500- to 1,000-member national association with an active local chapter.
    - ○ Once you have selected an industry, you may be able to identify the best organization to join simply by asking your connections in that industry which they would recommend.

- ❑ Contact them or visit their website to learn more about their members and request a membership kit.

The Ultimate Law Firm Associate's Working-from-Home Marketing Checklist

- ❑ If the membership includes legal-hiring decision makers, consider joining the group.

- ❑ Don't worry if the members are junior or mid-level professionals; build relationships with them when you're both early in your careers. They'll be able to start choosing their own lawyers when you're in a position to get hired.

- ❑ Validate that group with your contacts who know it.

- ❑ Once you have chosen the organization, your ultimate goal is to become one of the "influencers" in that group—a highly visible, friendly, helpful, active contributor. No pressure; plan to spend a couple years just learning about the industry and the association members. You're not selling yet, you're building your network, reputation, visibility, and credibility. This will pay off handsomely *later*.
  - ○ Attend at least 8 out of 12 monthly local chapter meetings per year, once we're back in the office.
  - ○ Network regularly and actively; get to know everyone.

- ❑ Keep the conversations focused on *them*.
  - ○ Remember the 80/20 Rule of Communication:
    - You should spend 20% of the time talking, mostly asking interested, insightful questions about them and their businesses, and 80% of the time listening.
  - ○ Remarkably, studies show that the more they talk, (1) the smarter they think you are, and (2) the more they like you!
  - ○ Be actively interested in them.

- ❑ Join a committee and follow through on any assignments or responsibilities.

- The highest-profile committees are Programming and Membership.
- People will judge your legal skills based upon how you perform as a volunteer. Do you meet your deadlines and commitments?

❑ Do not seek work or sell your firm, or you will be shunned as an <ugh> "vendor."

❑ Try to understand "why they buy," not "how to sell to them."

When I got started in marketing, our profession's organization was the national Legal Marketing Association (LMA), with 300 members. Working in-house as a large firm's Marketing Manager, I was one of the few lawyers in the organization. I discovered that I had something to contribute, that my knowledge of the law was helpful, so I wrote some articles for the local chapter and gave some speeches. They were well received, and I began to be invited to write and speak nationally. I was surprised to discover that I enjoyed it.

Within a few years, I realized that without even trying, I knew almost everyone in the entire national association. More importantly, they knew *me* as a helpful, trusted member of the legal marketing community. I'd dedicated my external communications activities toward a relatively small and finite group, just 300 people—half the size of my high school graduating class.

Over time, I just kept writing and speaking and networking. Writing and speaking and networking. Writing and speaking and networking. I later was invited to become the LMA's President but accepted the vice president role, which further increased my visibility. None of this was especially complicated or challenging; it was just the basic blocking and tackling that anyone can do.

Eight years later, when I left the law firm to go into consulting and needed to get hired by law firms, the LMA had grown to 3,500 members, and I found that I knew most of them, or at least they'd frequently read my articles and seen me speak. I had a national network of thousands of prospects who knew what I did and had a generally positive impression of me and my expertise.

I'd built this network entirely inadvertently. And with some basic planning and regular execution, absolutely anyone can do this on purpose.

Watson Bennett's idea of a branch office.

The lawyers of Watson Bennett spend a great deal of time in the woods. Not literally of course, but by advising clients in such timber- and forestry-related issues as litigation, energy and recreational leasing, land use, tax issues, warranty and title matters, boundary and easement issues, and all other complex issues facing the timber and forestry industries.

Contact Dave Colligan at 716.852.3540 or at dcolligan@watsonbennett.com to learn how we'll go out on a limb for you every day.

Learn more at www.ForestryLaw.com.

WATSON BENNETT
ATTORNEYS AT LAW

We never get lost in the woods.

Watson Bennett Colligan & Schechter LLP 12 Fountain Plaza Buffalo, NY 14202

www.watsonbennett.com

Noland Hamerly.
Our lawyers really know agriculture.

For 75 years our lawyers have handled every legal issue facing the agriculture industry. If agriculture is your business we should be your law firm. Noland Hamerly and Agriculture.

Together we grow.

NOLAND
HAMERLY
ETIENNE
& HOSS

333 Salinas Street
Salinas, CA 93901

Tel: 831-424-1414
www.lettucelaw.com

OUR LAWYERS' STRENGTH COMES FROM
DOING WHAT'S RIGHT.

If you have had a catastrophic injury, you can be sure our lawyers will move heaven and earth to make sure justice rules the day. Simple and true.

SCHLAPPRIZZI
REPRESENTING INJURED CATHOLICS

Leasing aircraft doesn't have to be done on a wing and a prayer.

VEDDER PRICE

We don't need to show you another picture of a plane. But Vedder Price knows the big picture in aircraft finance. We do sophisticated deals for every type of major asset across the U.S. and around the world in transportation industries including aircraft, maritime and rail. Multi-billion-dollar deals for every type of entity from airline lenders to lessors have cemented our reputation as one of the world's foremost transportation-finance practices. Learn more at vedderprice.com. **Vedder Price. Vedder Equipped.**

Chicago | New York | Washington, D.C. vedderprice.com

Is this ☐ a family pet
☐ the beneficiary of your father's entire estate

MacLEAN Estate Litigation

More Activities for Fourth- and Fifth-Year Associates

- ❏ Identify a **client development mentor**, ideally a young rainmaker who's invested in your future and can help answer questions and provide guidance and support. This person will also serve as an accountability partner to help you achieve your marketing goals.

- ❏ Learn about your clients' and prospects' companies and industries.
    - Regularly read industry websites, publications, and blogs.
    - Conduct online research periodically to stay current on their issues and needs.
    - Browse company websites regularly, especially sections like "About Us," and "News"
    - Follow them on social media.
    - If your firm has a Competitive Intelligence team, work with them to leverage firm tools like Manzama Insights to learn more about your target companies and decision makers.
    - Create a Google Alert for each company and important decision maker.

- ❏ Update significant matters you have worked on in your experience- or knowledge-management system. Also work with your marketing and business-development professionals to learn about the key details that help matters stand out in rankings, awards, and RFPs and include that information in your write ups. These activities will help raise your profile with others in the firm who might not have had the chance to work with you yet.
    - See "How to Write Persuasive Case Studies" in the Addendum.

- This may be a good time to review and update your biography to ensure that it shows your move from junior to mid-level associate.

☐ Notify your firm's marketers of significant cases and/or transactions you are involved in or are aware of, or anything novel you experience related to COVID-19 or working at home, etc. for media and public relations purposes.
  - Basically, if you ever find yourself saying, "Really??? *That's interesting!*" about some non-privileged information, your next thought should be "I'm going to tell Marketing about this! Perhaps we can use it to generate some publicity or attract some positive attention for the firm."

☐ Tweet at least weekly on issues relevant to your narrow area(s) of interest in normal times. These days, try to do so more frequently, to stay even more visible.

☐ Write an article for a legal or industry publication or blog on new issues, trends, or precedents relevant to your area(s) of interest.
  - Ask to include your photos(s), which will enhance your networking and brand.
  - Invite a client or hot prospect to co-author it with you, as a nice value-add.
    - Most likely, you'll do 90% of the work.
    - Later, frame a reprint and give it to the client over a follow-up lunch. It'll hang on their office wall, with your face on it.
  - Another option is to use the article as an opportunity to get a call or meeting with a valuable prospect.

- "I'm writing an article on XYZ and I need to quote an expert on this topic. Could I interview you for the article? The readers would find it valuable to have an in-house lawyer's [or business executive's] perspective in this."
- This is a great way to meet and do a nice favor for important executives.
  - This is just the first contact. Remember, it could take a dozen more before they would potentially be willing to send you some business. It's a marathon, not a sprint.
  - Continue regularly through partnership.

- ❏ I've always felt that it's more efficient to get some outside writing assistance to help push content out the door more efficiently. Lawyers have an enormous amount of useful information in their heads that would make interesting articles and blog posts. But few have the time or inclination to sit down to do the actual writing. Many find a blank screen daunting, so in spite of their good intentions, few actually get around to writing that article they planned.
  - Heather Morse, Chief Business Development Officer of McGlinchey, says "For years I have been very anti-ghost writing. No more. Content is king and we have to move it quickly from the attorney's mind to digital. We have contracted with a writer who is interviewing our attorneys and preparing a first draft of a blog post or article. It saves hours of time and is authentic because it starts and ends with our lawyers' voices."
  - Be careful with ghostwriters who want to generate articles under your name *without* having you provide that initial input. Some might consider that to be "misleading" and an ethical violation under Rule 7.1.

The Ultimate Law Firm Associate's Working-from-Home Marketing Checklist

- ❏ "If you are participating in a committee, develop content that can be shared with the membership online regarding strategies or news related to the pandemic." — Kathleen Flynn
  - Reach out to your committee members to check in on them.
  - Find out if the bar association is planning any webinars that fit your expertise and, if so, volunteer to participate as a moderator or panelist.
  - Add more examples of expertise to your resume and LinkedIn profile.

- ❏ "If you are a committee leader, rather than postponing your monthly meetings, host your next meeting as scheduled via video conference.
  - If your committee's business is on hold pending future events, you can still get the group together to stay connected.
  - Most of us take on these volunteer roles in order to meet people (not because we love stuffing nametags). So, don't let current events shut down your ability to build relationships.
  - Ask attendees to talk about how the coronavirus is impacting their businesses. Encourage people to share what they are doing to stay productive.
  - "Think of creative ways your group can support the larger organization or a community cause during this time." — Lydia Bednerik Neal

- ❏ Give an online presentation to a legal, industry, or community association or at an in-house client seminar.

- Carefully select the topic, using it to support your chosen niche or specialty practice. Now that physical conferences have been canceled, much of this programming will be pushed online. There will be a *lot* of webinars on hot topics presented by law firms, associations, vendors, and related companies.
- Your targets are already becoming saturated with webinar invitations and increasingly selective about which programs they sign up for, and quickly exit out of boring or unhelpful programs.
- Your goal shouldn't be to simply give a nice, educational program—it's to give the speech that the audience will remember next week.
- Always aim high and strive to give the best darn speech or webinar presentation possible. Be the presentation that every attendee will be talking about next week.
- If you enjoy speaking, seek to build a reputation as a strong presenter; there aren't many lawyers who can be both substantive *and* entertaining.
- Strong presenters build their reputation quickly.
  - Even if yours isn't the best speech, the attempt will improve the quality significantly.
  - You're likely to get invited back again, and word will spread around the industry.
- Create the follow-up activities ahead of time. For example, offer to send select PowerPoint slides or a topical article or checklist or a free hour of related legal advice to anyone who leaves a business card or contacts you later.
  - The goal is not to "give a presentation." A speech is an opportunity to build or reinforce your brand and create the first positive touch with a new group of potentially

The Ultimate Law Firm Associate's Working-from-Home Marketing Checklist

- interested buyers whom you can seek to convert into clients over time.
- **Audiotape and transcribe the speech** or use voice-recognition software. Most webinar platforms offer the option to record the program.
  - This single transcribed speech can be repurposed into dozens of different-length articles and blog posts for various audiences.
  - Edit the transcription into dozens of tweets and social media updates.
  - Professional editors can do much of this work for you, if you have a marketing budget.
- *"Here's the 10,000-word transcription of my speech. Please edit this into 100 tweets, 10 blog posts, one 5,000-word article, three 1,250-word articles, and five 500-word articles."*
  - Get professional presentation training. Public speaking is a learned skill.
  - Rehearse, rehearse, rehearse.
  - Practice the technology enough to become extremely comfortable with it.
  - In conference presentations, ensure you are videotaped, and review it afterward. (It can be mortifying to watch, but it's the best way to improve.)
  - Continue presenting through partnership.
  - Invite a client to co-present with you, as a nice value-add.
- Most likely, you'll do 90% of the prep work.

☐ Use this speech as the foundation of a wide range of material you will reuse, repurpose, and republish, spreading it across the Internet. See the video at *goo.gl/gf9eHF*

- Using a smartphone and portable tripod, videotape your presentation.
    - Upload the entire speech to Vimeo.com.
    - Trim the speech into as many quality 2- to 3-minute snippets as possible, and upload each of them to YouTube as individual videos, perhaps once every week or two. Create a strategic coordinated distribution schedule.
    - Use narrow, detailed keywords and industry buzzwords in the captions, tags, and descriptions so Google will index them thoroughly.
- Upload the PowerPoint slides to slideshare.net.
    - Create a thorough, detailed professional SlideShare profile.
    - Google highly ranks SlideShare profiles in name searches.
    - Connect the SlideShare .pdf to your LinkedIn profile.
- Post links and updates of your videos and slides to LinkedIn, Twitter, Facebook, and other social media accounts.
- If you're committed to speaking, hire a video editor to turn your speeches into a demo video.
- For example, my speaker video is online at t.ly/Dj5Y

❑ Collaborate with your firm's Marketing Department professionals.
- For now, arrange monthly 20-minute calls over lunch. When back at work, identify one of them with whom you have a positive connection and invite them out to lunch once per quarter to get advice.

❑ Learn how to produce and leverage client information and competitive intelligence.
- There's an abundance of valuable information available.

The Ultimate Law Firm Associate's Working-from-Home Marketing Checklist

- Use your firm library as a resource to help access competitive-intelligence information.
- Smart attorneys and firms understand how to leverage the power of critical information.

☐ Continue adding to your social network with friends and close professional contacts.
  - Update your plan to regularly connect with your list of top clients, prospects, and referral sources.
  - You should have a relatively robust list by now, and it's important to stay in front of them regularly, particularly during times of self-isolation.
  - Calling weekly is much too aggressive under normal circumstances but, in times of intense change, it can be appreciated, as long as you're regularly adding value.
  - Be a trusted advisor; bring them fresh ideas that help solve their latest problems. Work through their issues with them.
    - We're starting to see [this] in many companies like yours. Are you experiencing this too? Here are some of the ways we're addressing this with them. Does this make sense with your company too?
    - You know their industry, so help them understand what their competitors are doing to solve the same or similar issues. Raise those issues; they might not have thought of them. As the lawyer who helped identity the issue, you are in the best position to get hired to solve it for them. It also showcases you as the lawyer who helps them look around the corner for future concerns, positioning you as a trusted advisor. — Dave Bruns

☐ "Call clients and referral sources to check on them. Do they need anything (and not related to your services at all)? Take your time and really listen to them. Don't feel that you have to 'fix' their problems. Being a sympathetic ear is often enough." — Lydia Bednerik Neal

❑ Business or economic change frequently creates the need for new legal services. Be innovative, think creatively. What will the changing conditions mean for your targets? How can you help them get through this in a stronger position? Be creative and you'll find legal work amidst the chaos.
    ○ Ensure you update your biography to reflect this additional change or addition to your practice.

❑ "This is not business as usual. Many of your clients and prospects are experiencing the most difficult challenges in their personal and professional lives.
    ○ "Your tone should be concerned but reassuring.
    ○ "Make it easy for your clients to be in communication with you, not necessarily contingent on a particular transaction. Offer a specific value before you ask for anything or promote your services.
    ○ "Seek to be useful, not just available." – David Ackert
    ○ "Many of their issues may be *personal,* not professional, e.g. 'My kid's at home all day, and I'm now also a middle-school teacher, my parents are in their 80's and two states away, my college kid is in South Africa on a semester-abroad program and I can't get her home. How does this Zoom thing work?' Or 'I live in a 1,000-square-foot apartment and am now on top of my roommates all day long, and our Internet connection is slow.'" — Dave Bruns

❑ With information coming in fast and furious related to COVID-19, such as state-wide shelter-in-place orders and rapidly changing regulations, offer to develop a mechanism for tracking and updating orders and regulations, and share with your clients.

- ❑ When possible, engage in at least one face-to-face marketing effort per week, such as breakfast, lunch, dinner, drinks, sports, social event, seminar, conference, or association meeting. For now, try to reach out to a few people online every day. Something as simple as:

  > *Your name popped up on LinkedIn.*
  >
  > *How's it going? Every day I try to look for a few people I haven't spoken with in a while, just to say "Hello" and see if there's any way I can help enhance their success.*
  >
  > *I know business is challenging right now; is there something I can do to help you? If so, please do not hesitate to ask; it would be my pleasure to help you work through these tough times.*
  >
  > *Warmest regards,*
  > *Ross*

- ❑ Consider hiring a professional presentation consultant, particularly one who specializes in online presentations. A few quick tips:
  - ○ Be aware of how you look "In the box," i.e. the square you'll be framed in during your webinar.

More Activities for Fourth- and Fifth-Year Associates

- How's the lighting? Are you backlit and in silhouette? Perhaps you need to change locations or buy a soft light that will fill in your face, e.g. t.ly/qmB39
- Double-check the background behind you. Is it highly professional without distracting items? Zoom has a feature that lets you blur your background or replace it with a picture of something neutral. Don't rely on it; it looks like an amateurish green screen.
- It's important to make eye contact with the viewers, which means maintaining constant eye contact with a cold, impersonal camera lens. To make this easier, I tape a friendly photo of someone smiling at me immediately under the lens or attach a Post-It note with some eyeballs drawn on them. Trust me, it's much easier to have something to make eye contact with.
- "It's important, but *very* difficult to not look at your screen (instead of the camera) when someone on the screen is talking to you. Most younger people understand this, won't care, and will be looking at their screen too. Less tech-savvy or more traditional people will have more trouble if the other party doesn't seem to be looking at their face." – Andrew Fishman
- Sequester your pets far away so there's no cat walking across the keyboard or dog barking in the background. I give my dog a new chew toy and lock her in the other side of the house.
- Arrange care for any young children; a child with a boo-boo does not respect closed doors. See t.ly/yZJLG
- Dave Bruns suggests that in these difficult times, these personal issues are not considered as problematic as they would be under normal circumstances. In fact, he believes that it can help humanize you in

The Ultimate Law Firm Associate's Working-from-Home Marketing Checklist

your professional relationships and recommends addressing this issue up front: "We know everyone is at home and we might see some cats, dogs, kids, spouses, or doorbell from the delivery guy. Don't worry about it, we'll work through those issues…"
- Practice extensively with the software before the program so you can effortlessly take audience chatbox questions, watch the clock, and minimize the glitches.

☐ Offer to host a meeting at the firm for a group you're active in once we all get back to work. We'll all be glad to have the chance to meet and mingle again. Seek approval, or at least learn how to implement this within firm procedures.

☐ Volunteer to help organize or host your law school's fifth-year reunion.
- It's a great way to stay visible with hundreds of referral sources nationwide.
- Repeat for subsequent reunions.
- Arrange a regular series of Zoom calls to connect with your classmates. Becoming the center of the social connections will permanently maintain your friendly visibility with hundreds of potential referral sources.

☐ Create a Facebook and LinkedIn group for your law school class if one does not already exist. If there is one, join it and be active.
- Visibly moderate it, seeking fun photos, discussing memories, etc.
- Build your name recognition

Sixth Plus-Year Associates

MINDSET:

Start demonstrating that you're ready for partnership.

Stay in touch with and provide value to clients.

Share successes with contacts.

Enhance external profile and increase visibility.

Work with a practice-group leader or mentor to set annual business-development goals. Continue the activities listed above, supplemented with additional activities. If you haven't previously done much marketing, it's not too late, just start at the first chapter and accelerate the schedule. You may have a lot to accomplish, but it's not impossible; just stay focused and diligent.

- Meet with contacts at other professional-services firms if relevant to your practice niche (e.g. accounting, financial services, real estate, management consulting, public relations) to identify strategic-partnership opportunities such as co-hosted events, client teams, and referrals.
  - Follow-up to events and meetings is critical.
  - Having these calls via Zoom or Skype is entirely appropriate.

- Amber Naslund, Senior Content Consultant at LinkedIn offers sage advice regarding maintaining moderation in your use of teleconferencing: "Keep yourself and your colleagues sane.
  - "Not every call needs to be a video call now. Truly. Give people a break from having to constantly be in front of a camera to try to replace in-person engagement. It's different, and it can be draining.
  - "Please don't schedule your team (or yourself) back to back to back. It's tempting to try to fill all of this 'extra' time with work and grab that last 30-minute slot on someone's calendar, but that's not going to end well. Give everyone some breathing room.
  - "We're going to have to be in this for the long haul, so preserving some stamina for all of this intensity is going to be critical."

- Unless your practice area is driven primarily through lawyer referrals (e.g., litigation boutique, appellate, personal injury, divorce, patent, admiralty, white collar, insurance coverage), reduce your bar association activities and instead surround yourself with prospects, rather than competitors.

- ☐ Work toward a leadership position in your selected industry association.
  - ○ Consider running half-page ads in the industry publication and/or website homepage banners or direct emails, if:
    - You would be the only law firm advertising there, and
    - You can make the ads visually interesting enough to truly stand out. *See t.ly/pZJGk*

- ☐ Be helpful; offer advice and assistance.
  - ○ Jordan Goodman, a Senior State and Local Tax Partner at Chicago's Horwood Marcus & Berk, recommends mixing work and personal emails in his communications with his audience: "I have been sending out technical updates on State tax ramifications of the coronavirus. But in between, spaced a couple days apart, are 'funner' emails. The first was 'Top 10 tips for Working Remotely' and then today '10 humorous memes and stories about working remotely.' I got some thanks for the 'working remotely' list and the technical updates (now everyone is doing those). But the funny emails have elicited by far the most responses... which allows me to follow up with 'how's it going?' 'Whatcha working on?' or 'Let me know how I can help' or 'let me send you something on that.' Those are the golden opportunities for business development."

- ☐ Use technology to help grow and stay in touch with your network, e.g., blogs, Twitter, LinkedIn, etc.

- ○ Keep your platform narrow and *focused*. The world doesn't need another general "Litigation" or "Coronavirus Update" blog or Twitter feed.

- ❑ Request professional LinkedIn Recommendations, as appropriate.
  - ○ Write Recommendations for clients and prospects.

- ❑ Engage in at least two face-to-face marketing efforts per week when possible.
  - ○ For now, reach out to 3-5 online contacts via LinkedIn every day. Make one phone call to a client or hot prospect every day with a new idea or specific offer to help.

- ❑ Ask your partners and business development professionals to allow you to join them on pitches and client-assessment visits when appropriate.
  - ○ Once we're back to work, these face-to-face meetings will be especially important. The longer we're "sheltering in place," the more meaningful they will feel.

- ❑ If your small firm pays for martindale.com or lawyers.com profiles, seek both Peer and Client Ratings/Reviews (research.lawyers.com/lawyer-ratings.html)

- ❑ Visit clients on-site at their offices, factories, facilities, or stores, at no charge.
  - ○ Many rainmakers consider client visits to be the single most-important, most-effective marketing tool available.
  - ○ Dress appropriately for the location (suit, or jeans and work boots).
  - ○ Tour the plant, meet employees.

- Prepare for this visit. Research the client before you go, understand what your firm is doing for them holistically as well as what other firms they might be using for things like litigation or transactions. Ask insightful, educated, well-researched questions.
  - Become more familiar with their industry's legal and business issues.
  - This is critical: You are there to enhance your relationship and learn how to represent them better; DO NOT SELL.
  - Offer to do this as soon as we get the all-clear and are back at work and caught up. They will be facing enormous challenges at that time. These changes can create significant opportunities for them, and they will value the helpful advice of an experienced lawyer. This can help cement your relationship and lead to additional legal work.

- [ ] If you enjoy Twitter, follow the journalists who cover your practice area or industry.
  - Engage with them occasionally.
    - Build relationships with journalists who may ask you to act as a resource for articles.
    - Offer to provide expert commentary on cases or current legal developments.
  - Others who follow those journalists may follow you too.
    - Twitter is a geometric, not linear, platform.

- [ ] Learning basic PR skills isn't especially difficult.
  - Lawyers who understand how to use the media to their advantage can expedite their marketing success.
  - Two brief "PR for Lawyers" videos:
    - A 3-minute clip discussing what PR is and how it differs from other types of marketing, at *t.ly/eZPyn*

- A 10-minute clip discussing what makes something newsworthy, at *t.ly/1xn35*

☐ Talk to your marketing professionals regarding the analytics from your client alerts and blog posts and how you can use the information for business-development purposes.

☐ Write multiple versions of your elevator pitch.
    - Quick version: One or two sentences that describe what you do and why.
    - Medium version: One to two paragraphs; an expansion of your quick version of the what and the why to include the who.
    - Long version: An expansion of your medium version; can include example clients, representative engagements, and other relevant information
    - Alternative versions: Create customized versions of your elevator pitch for different audiences
    - Most importantly, a "canned" pitch isn't likely to be helpful. The goal is to ask the other person about themselves *first*. This way, when they then ask what *you* do, you will have the information that helps you describe yourself and your practice in an advantageous way, showing them that you are knowledgeable about their business and industry.
        - Why waste time talking about things you do that they don't care about?

☐ If your marketing activities have been adversely impacted by COVID-19 resulting in conference cancellations and other planned in-person events, consider reinvesting those dollars later in the year for client visits.

Social Media Tools

LinkedIn

LinkedIn currently has over 610 million members, with 303 million active monthly users, 40% of whom visit the site daily. Ninety-million senior-level influencers and 63 million decision makers use LinkedIn (cite).

According to the 2016 ABA Legal Technology Survey report, more than 93% of lawyers surveyed use LinkedIn. It hasn't quite taken off as a communication platform, but it's the foundation of most professionals' personal marketing. It's where you'll post articles and updates to your growing network.

Today, nearly everyone you would want to hire you, from Hiring Partner to client, will first skim your LinkedIn profile to learn more about you. So, make it persuasive, personal, and professional. Show them that you're more than a dispassionate one-page resume. This is your opportunity to help your targets see how wonderful you are and how lucky they'd be to have you on their team.

- ❏ If you don't have a **LinkedIn** page already, create one that is robust and can appeal on a variety of levels to a broad base of readers. This will be your most-important social media platform.
    - Draft a detailed LinkedIn personal profile.
        - Write in the first person with a friendly, professional tone.
    - If you already have one, now is a good time to update your page.
    - Don't identify yourself as "Partner at XYZ Firm" in the heading space. Consider this your attention-grabbing headline—intrigue your visitors with something dif-

ferentiating, using keywords that prospects searching for a lawyer on LinkedIn might use.
- Infuse it with your vibrant personality.
    - "Craft a summary that speaks not just to the work you do but who you are as a person, including charitable and volunteer work whenever possible." — Lisa Vicine
    - Ensure there are no typos. Zero. None.
        - A single typo could be disqualifying.
        - Have a friend proofread it for you.

- [ ] Build a sizable LinkedIn network, work toward hundreds of connections.
    - Start by connecting with people you know personally such as family, friends, peers, acquaintances, referral sources and classmates from all your schools.
    - Your goal is to get to 500 connections as soon as possible. Once you hit 500 connections, LinkedIn just shows "500+" on your profile. This works as social proof to others that you have an established professional network.
        - Join your law school LinkedIn group, and connect with anyone you know.
        - Consider starting a group for your graduation class.
    - Once you have a complete profile and established network you can start reaching out and connecting with professors, speakers you've heard at events, individuals who work at firms you are interested in, etc. Please feel free to connect with me as well.

- [ ] Fill it out completely, including the Contact Information and Education sections.
    - The two most-important areas are Summary and Experience.

- The Summary section is the very first thing people will read after your name and headline.
- The Experience section is where you get the opportunity to highlight all the exciting ways you have built up your personal brand, professional experience, and target niche (that I will be teaching you to do in the following chapters)
- Read the "How to Write a LinkedIn Profile" form in the Addendum.

❑ Add a quality photograph.
- An inexpensive passport photo from Walgreens will suffice.
  - You should dress similar to how you would look at a professional networking event.
  - Smile. Look like someone they might want to work with.
- No cropped vacation, party, wedding, or group photos.
- Nothing cute, grainy, badly lit, far away, or blurry. No pets or props. Be smart.
- "Research shows that having a photo makes your profile 14 times more likely to be viewed." — Lisa Vicine

❑ If you have an existing LinkedIn page, do a thorough audit to ensure it is highly professional.
- Delete anything the most-conservative grey-haired employer could possibly find offensive.
- Be judicious in what you include.
  - Delete all items from high school.
  - Be sensible regarding college activities.
- Write in the first person and use a friendly, casual tone.
- Create a custom public profile URL, so it's not random letters and numbers.

- Learn how by going to t.ly/5PIGE
  - Review the privacy settings for your profile. You want your profile to be Public so that people can see and connect with you. However, it is important to keep in mind that anything you "like" or "comment" on will be visible to anyone in your network, so use discretion.

- ❏ Like, join, or follow professional groups within your chosen specialty area.
  - Show your commitment to this industry or practice.

- ❏ Post occasional relevant updates, including thought-leadership pieces you will be writing in your chosen area of specialization/focus.

- ❏ It's easy to start by sharing or liking things that others in your specialty area have posted.
  - This will also visibly reinforce your commitment to this area.
  - Remember, listening and engaging with what others post is as important, if not more important, in social networking as what *you* say and post.

- ❏ No one expects your profile to be very long; just write simply and proficiently.

- ❏ Update it regularly, *at least* every few months, especially when your career is developing.
  - Ideally you should update it every time you publish an article, give a presentation, join a new committee, etc.
  - Check it at least weekly.

❏ Regularly "Endorse" classmates, friends, and peers; it only takes a *click*. They'll typically endorse you back.
  o Create evidence that you are well-liked, a leader among your group.
  o A word of caution with Skills and Endorsements: When you receive an endorsement from someone for a specific skill, only post it on your bio if you have actual expertise in that area. Some state bar rules have restrictions on this.
    • When in doubt, leave it off.

❏ Note that anyone whose LinkedIn profile you visit will receive a notification that you'd been there.
  o You can turn this off and browse in <u>Private Mode.</u>

Twitter

Twitter is a simple, quick, efficient platform to connect yourself to your specialty area online. Just 280 characters including spaces — a couple casual sentences and hashtags. It is an ideal communications platform to help build your brand and contact with others in a specialty area or industry niche.

- ❏ If you don't have a Twitter account, create one under your name.
  - For example, I'm @rossfishman (follow me!).

- ❏ Consider utilizing Twitter as a *listening* platform to better understand your specialty area, clients, prospects, competitors, scholars, and more.
  - Pay attention to what they are promoting, discussing, and commenting on. It can all be valuable.

- ❏ "Make sure to keep your private Twitter account separate from your professional Twitter account. You will not want your professional Twitter account to reflect any of your personal opinions, perspectives, or preferences that could alienate or offend existing and potential clients. Keep your professional Twitter posts just that … professional." — Lisa Vicine
  - Other marketers recommend using one single Twitter account for both personal and professional purposes. This would mean tempering your personal posts to ensure they are always appropriate for your professional audience as well.

- ❏ Check it at least once a week during normal times, and *daily* while self-isolating.

- ❏ Build your Twitter network; connect with your peers, professors, industry contacts, and thought leaders.
  - Follow people, companies, associations, and organizations within your legal, business, and specialty niche areas of interest.
  - I would encourage you to follow the marketers and other professionals who contributed to this book as well.

- ❏ Tweet at least weekly on issues relevant to your narrow area(s) of interest in normal times. These days, try to do so more frequently, to stay even more visible.
  - Remember to include the narrow search engine optimized (SEO) keywords that the media and experts in this industry or area would use to search.
  - Ensure you learn the nuances of the jargon.
  - Posts with photos or graphics get significantly greater attention.

- ❏ Re-tweet the tweets that resonate with you, to help grow your network.

- ❏ If you enjoy Twitter, follow the journalists who cover your practice area or industry.
  - Engage with them occasionally.
    - Build relationships with journalists who may ask you to act as a resource for articles.
    - Offer to provide expert commentary on cases or current legal developments.

- ❏ If you enjoy using Twitter as a social media platform:
  - Check it occasionally.

- Build your Twitter network; connect with contacts, clients, and thought leaders.
- Post at least weekly on something relating to your job or interests.
- Retweet tweets that resonate with you.
- Consider utilizing Twitter as a *listening* platform to better understand clients, prospects, competitors, scholars, and more.
- Pay attention to what they are promoting, discussing, or commenting on. It can all be valuable.
- Follow people, companies, associations, and organizations within your legal, business, and general areas of interest.
  - Others who follow them may follow you too.

Facebook

Consider Facebook to be a defensive strategy. You're unlikely to positively influence decision-makers using your personal Facebook profile, but an unfortunate post or photo could eliminate you from consideration. Don't risk it.

- ❏ Analyze your Facebook page. Do a detailed audit to sanitize it.
    - ○ Upgrade your privacy security settings to hide yourself from prying eyes.
    - ○ Delete any party photos, *etc*.
    - ○ Delete anything a conservative senior partner could possibly find offensive.
        - • If you wouldn't proudly show it to your grandmother, *delete* it.
    - ○ Keep it casual and sensible. This is a less-formal medium than LinkedIn.
    - ○ Consider creating a new public Facebook page as a platform to support the professional brand you're creating.
        - • Add occasional updates and photos of your specialty events, speeches, meetings, etc.
        - • You can post similar content here that you would post on LinkedIn.

- ❏ Consider creating a new public Facebook page as a platform to support the professional brand you're creating.
    - ○ Add occasional updates and photos of your specialty events, speeches, meetings, etc.
    - ○ You can post similar content here that you would post on LinkedIn.
    - ○ Connect with your friends, especially those from law school.

- Consider connecting with clients, prospects, and referral sources with whom you have a personal relationship.
- Join your law school class's Facebook group.
- Check it at least weekly in normal circumstances, more frequently when working from home.

YouTube

Video is increasing in popularity with lawyers seeking to spread their message; it can be a powerful marketing tool. YouTube is the second-most frequently used search engine, after Google.

❏ Hide, delete, or mark "Private" any videos that do not support your professional strategy and exemplify the type of persona you are trying to create.

❏ Be careful with any videos you like or comment on and what channels you follow because this could be visible to others as well.

❏ Create a new YouTube account for the short specialty videos you may soon be creating.

❏ You can shoot high-definition videos with your smartphone.
  - Buy an inexpensive tabletop tripod and spring-clip smartphone holder. You can find them online for $10.
  - No one expects cinema quality movies, but poor quality audio and lighting can destroy the impact of an otherwise valuable video. Invest in a high-quality external microphone and some soft lighting to fill in the shadows so you're not a dark silhouette, e.g. t.ly/qmB39
  - Consider creating a series of 1-3-minute videos that offer updates on hot topics in your areas of specialization or personal interest.
    - It's easier than you think; if you fumble your language, simply delete that video and start over.

- Help prospects find your videos. Carefully tag, caption, and describe them with the SEO-friendly keywords that prospects who are searching for useful content would use.

❏ Review the "Write, Speak, Repurpose, and Reuse" chapter below for ideas.

Instagram

As with Facebook, most business lawyers will want to use a defensive strategy with Instagram, although it seems to be growing in importance for firms marketing to a younger audience. It can be particularly effective for personal injury, criminal, and other firms that target lay consumers. Be aware that your personal profile may show up in a basic search of your name.

- ❑ Analyze your Instagram profile. Do a detailed audit to sanitize it.
    - ○ Consider making your profile private or change your Instagram name.
    - ○ Delete any party photos, *etc*.
    - ○ Delete anything a conservative senior partner could possibly find offensive.
        - If you wouldn't proudly show it to your grandmother, *delete* it.

Snapchat

Snapchat won't help you professionally, but it can hurt you. As with the other forms of social media, use good judgment about the content you create and share. You never know who is watching.

Business Cards

Business Cards

- ❑ When you're out, *always* have business cards with you. This is important, even when you're not attending business functions; you never know when you might meet someone who might turn into your next big client. Pre-2020, I presented at 30+ conferences per year. In my experience, roughly 20% of the attendees would have neglected to pack business cards. I don't remember any of them.

- ❑ They may seem old-fashioned to some, but they remain a vital part of today's networking, particularly with the older and more senior people.

- ❑ Cards remain the simplest, most tangible way for people to remember you and contact you later.

- ❑ Consider adding your LinkedIn profile URL and Twitter username (including the @ sign).

- ❑ Don't leave these business cards to gather dust in your bottom drawer; they can't help you unless they're with you. Here's how to guarantee you have cards when you need them:
  - Leave 75–100 in the box in your desk, then divide up the rest among all of your pants pockets, suit coats, blazers, jackets, overcoats, purses, gym bags, briefcase, backpack, suitcase, roller bag, and glove box.
  - Put a rubber-banded stack in your suitcase, so you don't forget them when you're traveling.
  - Watch this brief video about business cards at t.ly/dZmW6

The Ultimate Law Firm Associate's Working-from-Home Marketing Checklist

- ❏ Women's outfits may not have pockets.
    - ○ Plan for networking events by wearing a blazer with pockets.
    - ○ Ensure you have a purse with a shoulder strap and keep your cards in an outside pocket, so you can effortlessly pull them out with one hand.
    - ○ In a pinch, you can insert a few cards in the back of your plastic name tag, or in your cell phone case.

- ❏ At networking events, to avoid embarrassing mix-ups, always keep your own cards in your *left*-side pants or jacket pockets, and the cards you collect on your *right* side.

- ❏ The goal is not to simply pass out cards to attendees.
    - ○ You must collect their cards as well, to ensure that you can manage the flow of communications and effectively follow up with them.
    - ○ Do not put the burden on them to stay in touch.
    - ○ Read more under "Networking and Attending Seminars" below.

Networking and Attending Seminars

Networking and Attending Seminars

Since the COVID-19 outbreak, networking has moved online, but it remains the foundation of all business development. It's important to know how to network, particularly at conferences and seminars where you'll find a target-rich environment of prospects. Conferences have all been cancelled for health concerns but when we're eventually able to get together again, the following techniques can build your personal brand and reputation, and accelerate the development of the network of prospects who will become your future clients. It's worth reviewing the techniques you'll want to use, whether you're speaking or attending.

- ❑ Networking is a *long-term* process. Learn to meet more of the *right* people, those whom you can turn into prospects, business contacts, then clients.
    - ○ "Active listening" is important.
    - ○ Ask well-informed questions regarding their business.
    - ○ Listen for opportunities and ways to help them achieve their goals.
    - ○ Ask your firm to bring in training on networking skills. See the brief video at goo.gl/Bwq9ii
        - Networking is a learned skill. It's not difficult, but many behaviors seem counter-intuitive.

- ❑ ***Before* the Event**
    - ○ Determine whether the event you'll be attending is business or social.
        - If it's *social*, great, have fun. But if it's *business*, then you'll need to be more intentional and strategic, and invariably have less fun.
    - ○ When blocking off the event on your calendar, block off an additional hour in addition to the scheduled time.

The Ultimate Law Firm Associate's Working-from-Home Marketing Checklist

- Commit to arriving 30 minutes before the program starts and staying 30 minutes later—*that's* when the actual networking occurs, not during the presentation.
- If your goal is to create new relationships or reinforce existing ones, this extra networking time is important.
  - Consider doing some quick Internet research regarding any targets or prospects whom you expect to be at the event.
    - This information gives you an easy conversation starter ("Hey, I read that you were [doing X]. Tell me about that!"
    - It also positions you as the type of informed, educated professional they should want to work with.
  - Write down a few simple, tangible goals to complete. They can be simple, e.g. "Meet two new people," or "Collect three business cards," or "Speak with Amanda at ABC Company."
    - Identifying specific goals makes your behavior more strategic and intentional; it'll guide your movements and let you know if you've been successful.
    - One goal should be to speak with an existing contact you know will be there.
    - Ask two questions: "How's business?" and "What are you working on that you find especially interesting?"

- ☐ ***During* the Event**
  - **Be strategic regarding whom you speak to.** You're busy and you have taken valuable billable time away from work to be here.
  - You have only 30 minutes to meet and speak with the people you need to help advance your career. You can't afford to risk spending this time with the "wrong" people.

- Subtly read their name tag and assess whether they fit your strategic profile *before* approaching and engaging them in conversation. (Don't get caught doing it.)
    - It might feel a tad mercenary, but remember, you've decided that this is *business*. You're at this event to meet new people who might turn into prospects and clients, not to make friends. That's for some other time or event.
- Don't sit at empty tables. The same rule applies to where you sit—be deliberate regarding whom you'll spend lunch with.
    - Choose your seatmates carefully, intentionally, and subtly.
    - You'll spend an important hour between these two people. Make sure they're the "right" people for this occasion.
- Try to meet more, rather than fewer people.

❑ **Wear a name tag**
- If you need to write your own, make it neat, large, and legible. It helps attendees ask you questions and remember you later.
- Affix name tags to your *right* lapel, not your left. This way it faces towards people when shaking hands with them.
- Gender-communication expert Susan Freeman, President of Freeman Means Business, suggest that "Women may need to plan ahead regarding their fashion choices to avoid damaging fragile clothing with a name tag's sticker or clip.
    - "Have a selection of indestructible "conference blazers."

The Ultimate Law Firm Associate's Working-from-Home Marketing Checklist

- "Keep a blazer hanging on your door at work for last-minute programs."
  - If you're given a lanyard, position it above your chest so people can comfortably see it.
    - It may have a spring-clip to resize it. Tie a knot if necessary.
    - A name tag dangling around your stomach is entirely invisible. (These days, no one will risk being caught looking down there.)
  - When you next receive a magnetic-clip name tag, consider keeping it in your briefcase. They're the most flexible and least destructive style and can be reused in future events.

- ☐ **Networking Questions.** It can be difficult to get started in conversation with a stranger. Try some of these.
  - [Look at their name tag.] Tell me about [company].
    - What do you do there?
    - What kinds of products/services do you provide?
    - Who are your target customers?
  - How did you get started in _____?
  - What do you enjoy most about what you do/the topic of the event?
  - What changes are happening in your industry?
  - What are some of the projects you are currently working on?
  - What can I do to help you/your business?
  - Would you teach me more about _____ [business/topic they have an interest in]?

- ☐ **Graceful Exit.** Once you've made a good impression with someone within your target audience, create a relevant follow-up meeting or activity, commit to that follow-up, then

Networking and Attending Seminars

exit the conversation so you both can continue networking.
- It's socially acceptable to suggest that you need to make a call, use the restroom, say hello to someone you see across the room, or get a drink.
  - A friend of mine always orders a half-glass of beer at the bar. This way, he's never more than a few ounces away from an excuse to get out of an unhelpful conversation.
- "I don't want to take up all your time. "I'd like to continue our conversation, so how about we plan to get together? "I'll email you in the next couple days."
  - Then be sure that you *do* it.
- Write your promise on the back of their business card after you split up, so you'll remember.
- Don't get caught doing it, some people and cultures believe that writing on their business card is insulting.
  - Follow-up is hard. But it works.
- Don't monopolize their networking; they want to speak with more people too.
  - You must *force* yourself to keep moving. It's too easy to simply continue a positive conversation when things are going well.
  - Fight the urge to speak only to your friends. Hanging out with them is easy and fun, but that's not why you're at this event.

❑ ***After* the Event**
- Connect with them on LinkedIn within 24 hours, with a brief personal note that reminds them of who you are.
- Use the information on the business cards to add them to your firm's contact list or database for appropriate mailings, holiday cards, etc.

- ○ Try to send a follow-up email by the next afternoon. Keep it simple and to the point, such as, "Nice meeting you, let's continue our conversation over lunch."
    - Offer a specific date, time and place in your email. Don't waste time with endless noncommittal back-and-forth communications.
    - Be polite and assertive; they will appreciate your being direct.
- ○ Follow up as promised. For example, you might say, "After we spoke, I looked into [the topic in question] that relates to our conversation. I have attached a couple of the firm's electronic updates on this issue. Are you signed up to receive them?"

- ❏ While it's important to provide the client with as much meaningful information as you can, it's also important to find out as much as possible about their business and role.

- ❏ Clients particularly value lawyers who understand their business and industry. Speaking the client's language can set you apart in a positive way.

- ❏ Think about a strategy for the specific kinds of business initiatives and legal work on which you would like to partner with clients.

Conduct a "Needs Assessment"

Conduct a "Needs Assessment"

The basis for conducting this assessment is to identify the client's needs and objectives. It will also give you and the client the opportunity to work together to brainstorm and create a clear plan for the future.

The key is to strategize and present this information in a way that identify their questions and concerns and helps them achieve their future goals. If there are legal solutions to their concerns, you have a path to find a way to work together on them.

- ❏ Susan Freeman offers "some powerful questions that show respect for the client, giving them an opportunity to share what's most important to them, below:
  - From your perspective, what would be a valuable way for us to spend this time together?
  - What would be useful for you to know about our firm?
  - What prompted your interest in our meeting?
  - In talking to some of our clients in your industry, I'm struck by a couple of particular issues they are grappling with. These include: [give examples]. How would these resonate with you and your management?
  - How is your organization reacting to... (a recent, important development in this client's industry or function)?
  - How are you handling... (new competition, cheap imports, a new regulatory framework)?
  - Is there is a particular competitor you admire?
  - Can you tell me what your biggest priorities are for this year?
  - What are your most significant opportunities for growth over the next several years?
  - What exactly do you mean when you say ["risk-averse," "dysfunctional," "challenging?"]

The Ultimate Law Firm Associate's Working-from-Home Marketing Checklist

- Who would you say are your most valuable customers?
- What would your best customers say are the main reasons they do business with you?
- Why do customers stay with you?
- Why do customers leave?
- When customers complain, what do they say?
- How have your customers' expectations changed over the past five years?
- How would you describe the biggest challenges facing your own customers?
- What's the driving force behind this particular initiative? What is behind the drive to reduce costs, design a new organization, etc.?
- What would "better" (risk management, organizational effectiveness, etc.) look like?
- How much internal agreement is there about the problem and the possible solutions?
- From your perspective, given everything we've discussed, what would be a helpful follow-up to this meeting?"

☐ Any one of these can help you to show respect, gain trust, build rapport, and, ultimately, be likable.
  - Since people want to work with people they like, try *active listening,* rather than talking.

General Mindset

Always remember, whatever your job, **always do more than is expected.**

Clients can't often tell whether you're doing a good technical job, but they can tell how well you're treating them, and this is especially true when you can't physically shake their hand and look them in the eye. Communicate regularly. Meet your obligations and deadlines. Be responsive–don't make clients wait to hear from you. Try to return every call and email within two hours and never let a call or email go unreturned overnight. Don't be afraid to return a call or email simply saying you are working on it and giving the client a deadline when they can expect to receive the requested information.

Treat every person at the firm with the utmost respect regardless of their gender, race, religion, sexual orientation, age, or title. Learn the names of all of the receptionists, secretaries, clerks, and messengers, and *use* them. It's not only the decent thing to do, people notice. It matters. Savvy lawyers understand that secretaries and receptionists are often the best source of information because they have different guards up and might be more willing to share.

Gender-Based Communication Musings

Gender-Based Communication Musings

Susan Freeman offers some personal insight into gender-communications within law firms:

Women remain underrepresented at every level in corporate America, despite having earned more college degrees than men for over thirty years. Most organizations understand the need to do more—corporate commitment to gender diversity is at an all-time high. Nonetheless, progress remains slow—and may even be stalling.

One of the most-powerful explanations is the simplest—we have blind spots when it comes to diversity, and we can't solve problems we don't see or understand. Raise awareness in your own firm and lead by example. Women need to have an equal shot at the career-stretching assignments. To create equity in the workplace, we must help women and men communicate more effectively.

- Diversity and inclusivity are not the same things.

- Firms that are diverse and inclusive perform better than firms that are not.

- Diversity requires including women and men of different ages and races.

- Inclusivity calls for complete integration of all employees into all firm operations.

- Women and minorities benefit from having people who coach them on "political navigation" as well as skills development.

The Ultimate Law Firm Associate's Working-from-Home Marketing Checklist

In the workplace, people are continuously—and often unconsciously—assessing your communication style for two sets of qualities: warmth (empathy, likeability, caring) and authority (power, credibility, status). In all cases, a communication style turns into a weakness when overdone. A woman's collaborative approach can appear submissive and a man's directness can seem callous.

Men appear aggressive when their expansive postures infringe on other's personal space (sometimes called "manspreading"), when they have a "death grip" handshake, and when they emphasize status cues to the point where they look haughty and uncaring. Women are viewed as weak or passive when they are unnecessarily apologetic, when they smile excessively or inappropriately, and when they discount their own ideas and achievements.

Typically, women have the edge in collaborative environments where listening skills, inclusive of body language and empathy are highly valued, and are judged as better at dialogue. Women are more empathetic and less combative. Because they are better at listening, they can more effectively and consistently find client-centered solutions.

Without as much ego or bluster, they can find unique solutions to litigation, rather than just filing a lawsuit. Most clients want to avoid costly litigation, yet many male attorneys do not even consider seeking a creative solution or alternative. The client's real goal is to resolve the dispute and get back to making money. In this regard, a female attorney's inclination to listen and predisposition to be creative, offers a solid advantage.

Women are generally more patient and better listeners, positioning them to understand the client's real needs when negotiating a deal or trying to solve a client's business problem.

Research shows that success and likeability are positively correlated for men and negatively correlated for women. That is, when a man is successful, his peers often like him more; when a woman is successful, both men and women may like her less. This trade-off between success and likeability creates a double-bind for women. If a woman is competent, she does not seem nice enough, but if a woman seems really nice, she is considered less competent. This can constrain a woman's career advancement.

This bias often surfaces in the way women are described, both in passing and in performance reviews. When a woman asserts herself—for example, by speaking in a direct style or promoting her ideas—she is often called "aggressive" and "ambitious." Or worse. When a man does the same, he is considered "confident" and "strong."

According to Carol Goman, author of *The Silent Language of Leaders*, women display more "warm" body language cues. They are more likely to focus on those who are speaking by orienting head and torso to face participants. They lean forward, smile, synchronize their movements with others, nod and tilt their heads (the universal signal of listening, literally "giving someone your ear").

These are powerful and positive communication traits. Understanding these differences in gender-based communication give you an advantage. Use what you now know to grow and protect your practices, your client's company, and yourself.

The receiver makes meaning of the message—regardless of the sender's intent. Effective communication takes place when the sender confirms the message is received as the sender intended. For each person certain communication strategies are more effective than others. As men and women communicate differently, there are common practices that make building and maintaining relationships a bit easier. We suggest giving the following recommendations an old college try:

- ❑ Adapt to sudden changes in direction whether in your personal or professional life.

- ❑ Use an easy-going and, where appropriate, fun, approach to building and nurturing relationships with colleagues and clients.

- ❑ Be prepared to share problems openly with trusted advisors or mentors inside the firm.

- ❑ Provide information that stimulates conversation among people of differing personalities, views, and styles.

- ❑ Ask for others' thoughts and ideas—even if they conflict with your own.

- ❑ Don't always expect brief, specific answers, especially outside of the courtroom.

- ❑ Allow for storytelling—your own and that of others—in your life.

- ❑ Acknowledge unique talents and leadership skills, even when you are not the leader.

- ❑ Be clear on your expectations, desired outcomes and completion details.

- ❑ Support others' needs for new ideas, state-of-the-art technology, modern-day materials, and intellectual growth challenges.

- ❑ Offer others praise and appreciation when due, early and often.

- ❑ Indulge in occasional speculation, knowing sometimes the questions are more meaningful than the answers anyway.

Your Mental Health

Law can be a difficult and stressful career. We work long hours on intellectually and emotionally challenging projects for clients who may seem demanding and unappreciative. We bring the work home with us not just physically, but also mentally and emotionally. It is essential to take care of yourself. Eat right, get enough sleep and exercise, and spend time with your friends, family, and hobbies. Volunteer for a charity. Ensure you have a vibrant and fulfilling life outside of your practice, as well. Being successful and productive is more about that balance than it is about the quantity of work you have produced.

Law can be an isolating profession even while working in an energetic office. In today's uncertain times, it is important to focus on your emotional and mental well-being in addition to your physical condition. The "social-distancing" and "self-isolating" behaviors that can keep you free of disease can be lonely and stressful. These can cause additional health problems and aggravate any physical problems you may have.

During periods of intense and extended isolation, take the time to exercise and find productive ways to distract yourself. Try to maintain a consistent daily routine, even just waking up and eating at the same time every day. Take a walk or ride a bike. Do an art project or start a 1,000-piece puzzle.

Start some of the things you've been putting off, like cleaning out your drawers or closets. Take an online class and learn a new skill. Write that article or blog post that you've been thinking about. Learn to play the guitar; in just a few days you can be strumming and singing early Beatles with your friends online.

Sarah Tetlow suggests "when distracting projects pop into your mind or vision while you're trying to finish a deadline for work, quiet the distraction by identifying **when** you will address it.

- 'I need to do the laundry. I will do it when I take a break at 3:00.'
- 'I should write an article about this topic!' I will place a tickler reminder to prepare the draft on Tuesday after I've filed this brief.
- 'I would love to clean out that closet.' I will do that on Saturday afternoon.

By identifying a scheduled time for your next action on those precious thoughts and tasks, it will help calm your brain of the distraction knowing you have a plan."

Speaking of calming the brain, practice mindfulness with an app like *Calm* or *Headspace*. Listen to some stress-reducing music, like "Weightless," by Marconi Union. Use this time to get in better shape by downloading an exercise app like *Couch to 5K*, *Hundred Pushups*, or *Pocket Yoga*, and get started!

Andrew Fishman, LSW say "It's important to stay informed, but it's easy to become overwhelmed by too much bad news. Consider limiting the news to certain times of the day. Try to figure out how much information you need to make healthy choices without going overboard or obsessing.

"Resist the powerful attraction to the social media platforms that can increase your stress. Sites like Facebook often act as a funnel for bad news, fake news, conspiracy theories, and people either complaining about their miserable lives or humble bragging about how much better their lives are than yours.

"In times of crisis, people may worry about their loved ones getting sick and dying. This is often connected to the amount of media a person consumes. This fear isn't *entirely* irrational but may do more harm than good; stress like this can damage your mental and physical health. Unless it's helping to make healthy decisions, worrying isn't a good use of time.

"Try to be proactive about connecting with loved ones. Get as close as you can to meeting in person. That is, Facetiming is better than calling, because you can see the smiles on their faces. Calling is better than texting because it's more interactive and you can hear them laugh. And texting is more dynamic than passive email well-wishes. Share upbeat messages on Instagram.

"If you and your friends are into video games, try multiplayer games like *Super Smash Bros., Animal Crossing, Jackbox Games,* or *Overwatch* to spend time together. If your favorite multiplayer game doesn't have an in-game chat option, set up a Discord channel to keep open on the side. Just make sure to turn off public chat, if you can."

Consider reading *The Happiness Advantage* by Shawn Anchor, which discusses how "happiness fuels success." In your life and career, strive for a career that provides *both*.

If you feel that you may need some support or assistance, there are many available resources designed specifically for lawyers. These include (1) Lawyer Assistance Programs through state and local bar associations and (2) the renowned Hazelden Betty Ford Foundation at hazeldenbettyford.org/. Seek them out.

Conclusion

Conclusion

If you follow this checklist, over time you should find that you have developed a significant network of contacts you can turn into clients. Moreover, you will have laid the foundation for a successful career, one that is fulfilling personally, professionally, and financially.

Remember, once you identify what you love to do, find a way to bring that into your practice. If you do, you may spend your time until retirement leaping out of bed every morning absolutely passionate about your profession, your career, and your success.

Good luck!

Author Biography

Ross Fishman, J.D.

Of Counsel magazine wrote: "Many people consider Ross to be the nation's foremost expert on law firm marketing."

Ross is one of the legal profession's most popular marketing and ethics CLE keynote speakers. Often characterized as both highly entertaining and educational, Ross's presentations draw on his experience as a litigator, marketing director, and marketing partner, inspiring lawyers at all levels.

A Fellow of both the College of Law Practice Management and the Litigation Counsel of America (LCA), Ross has branded 200 law firms worldwide on six continents and has written 300 by-lined articles, including seven monthly columns. Selected as a "Lawdragon 100 Leading Consultants and Strategists, he received the international Legal Marketing Association's (LMA) first peer-selected Lifetime Achievement award and was the first marketer inducted into the LMA's international Hall of Fame.

A particular highlight was when a grateful Louisville law firm client had the Governor commission Ross as a Kentucky Colonel. He's been quoted in the media hundreds of times, in publications including *The Wall Street Journal, The New York Times,* and NPR's "All Things Considered."

A member of the federal Trial Bar (N.D. Ill.), Ross received a B.A. in Speech Communications, *cum laude*, from the University of Illinois, and his J.D. from Emory University School of Law. **Subscribe to his marketing blog** at *fishmanmarketing.com/blog*. His speaker website is rossfishman.com.

ross@fishmanmarketing.com
fishmanmarketing.com
rossfishman.com
LinkedIn.com/in/rossfishman
Twitter: @rossfishman

Addendum

NICHE AND INDUSTRY MARKETING CHECKLIST: LONG VERSION

Niche/Industry Marketing© Worksheet for Lawyers

What industry or niche specialty practice should you focus on?

Target companies must be appropriate to the size of the firm:

- What's your specialty niche?
- What type work do you want more of?
- Are there people/industries you particularly enjoy?
- What types of companies are most likely to hire you?

What skills, interest, or passion leads to an appropriate target?

- Something interesting/unusual about you?
- Previous job/career providing insight?
- Family business you worked in?
- Spouse's business you have contact in?
- Existing client providing industry experience?
- Previous big win/case study to get you started?
- Personal connections to give you a leg up?
- A hobby that engenders useful insight?

Select *one* industry group or trade association.

Browse through the *Encyclopedia of Associations (see page 47)* and select a little-known, niche-oriented trade or professional association upon which to focus your marketing efforts—ideally a national organization with a nearby local chapter where you can focus your monthly networking activities. Surround yourself with *clients*, not competitors.

- You must be active, visible.
- Attend monthly meetings.
- Join the membership committee.
- Work to leadership position.
    - Committee chair
    - Conference chair
- Focus most of your marketing activities on this group.
    - Networking, research, biography, articles, speeches, public relations, ads, etc.

Some ways to focus your practice, a health care example:

- **Geography:** "National" is usually too broad. Define a narrower geographic region.
- **Size of business:** Focus on a certain segment of the business (e.g. just small or large hospitals).
- **Type of business:** Subset of a larger industry (e.g. ambulatory care facilities).
- **Injury type:** Focus on a certain type of injury (e.g. punitive damages or emotional distress).
- **Practice area:** Specialize in a narrow area (e.g. kidney dialysis or anesthesiology).
- **Or a combination:** Select two among the list (e.g. radiology cases in small hospitals).

What do I do after identifying some likely organizations?

- Contact them; the information is in the *Encyclopedia of Associations*.

   > "I represent companies in your industry and would like to learn more about your association. Do you have a local chapter?"

- Request membership information.

- Learn about pricing, benefits, member demographics. Are they your target prospects?

- Analyze the conference schedule, magazines, and website.

What's the plan?

- "We don't accept [vendor] members."

   > "I can help members avoid trouble, protect themselves, save money...

- Write articles for magazine, newsletter

- Preventive-law monthly column

- Local/national conference speeches

- Network monthly at local meetings

- Advertise

Summary

Focusing your marketing clarifies your message and identifies how to use the standard tools most efficiently and effectively:

- Website
    - *Micro-site or blog* directly on point.
- Networking
    - *Finite audience* to meet.
- Research
    - *Specific industry* to learn about.
- Biography
    - *Tailored experience* to describe.
- Social media
    - *Add to LinkedIn bio.*
    - *Twitter* can establish expertise with the media.
- Brochure, print or electronic
    - *Targeted* to group's needs.
- Articles
    - *Focused message* is easy to discuss in print or on blogs.
- Speeches, Newsletters
    - *Interested audience* and a narrow topic.
- Public relations, quotes
    - *You're the expert,* so reporters need you.
- Advertising
    - *Inexpensive placement* in targeted publications or online.

NICHE/INDUSTRY MARKETING CHECKLIST: SHORT VERSION

Seek to identify one or more narrow niches in which, if effectively marketed, you could use to build a successful, focused practice. Where can you become a market leader? This form seeks to focus your thoughts regarding where to start.

Consider specific industries, narrow market segments, target communities, geographic regions, sub-practice specialties, and/or areas of narrow expertise. Avoid broad, traditional headings like Health Care, Real Estate, Insurance, Construction, or Financial Services. In what niche do you have the threshold level of expertise and limited law firm competition?

1. What narrow niche or industry should you consider targeting?

2. Identify any other firm lawyers who have experience in the target area.

3. Briefly describe your interest or expertise for this niche or industry.

4. Identify one or more existing clients or contacts in the targeted area.

5. Identify the best trade associations or similar organizations serving the target area, if you know (or look in Gale Publishing's *Encyclopedia of Associations*)

6. Identify any lawyers or firm(s) who would be your primary competitors.

7. How might you or the firm distinguish yourself from competing law firms in those areas?

INDIVIDUAL MARKETING PLAN: LONG VERSION

Describe Your Personal Marketing Goals for [year]

I. Developing Your Network and Reputation

Clients perceive professional activities like writing, speaking, and bar- and industry-association activities as indications of your knowledge and skill. Ensure clients know about your activities by sharing through the firm's marketing outreach, and posting to social media.

A. Networking

Networking is the foundation of client development. Build a network of the *right* contacts. After a thorough analysis, *precisely* identify the most likely sources of new business for the practice you are trying to develop—your "target audience." Next, find out which industry or trade associations they belong to and which meetings they attend. Then join those organizations and *work toward a leadership position.* You can't get business if the people who hand out the business don't know, trust, and respect you. This is a critical, *long-term* professional-development activity.

I will actively participate as a member of:

- ❏ **Industry or Trade Association(s)** In which *industry* would you like to develop contacts? What groups do your clients belong to?

- ❏ **Bar Association(s)** These help professional development and build a strong resume. For business-development purposes, it is better to be the only lawyer in a roomful of potential clients than sitting among other lawyers. Allocate your time carefully. As a young lawyer, select one bar association and work toward a leadership position. *Get active and visible!*

II. Developing Existing Client and Prospect Relationships

It is important to focus much of your marketing efforts on maintaining and expanding existing relationships.

A. Strengthening and Expanding Existing Client Relationships

Roughly 80% of a firm's new business comes from the top 20% of its clients. Lawyers should commit to strengthening, enhancing, and expanding these top relationships. The primary focus is to learn more about their businesses and industries, strategic business goals, and legal needs so that you can provide more informed and useful counsel. An added benefit of this enhanced understanding is that it positions you to identify new business opportunities. As the General Counsel of a Fortune 500 company said, "If you're not willing to take the time to learn about me, you do not really want my business." List the two current clients you will work to strengthen the firm's relationship with.

Existing Client's Name:

- ❑ **Company Research.** It is important to have current information about firm clients. To learn more about their company and industry so that I can serve them better, I will review their website, including the "What's New" section. I will leverage firm resources to learn more about my clients. (see *www.google.com/alerts*)

- ❑ **Client Visit (5th-year associates and up).** Within 6 weeks, I will volunteer to visit the client's facility, for free, to learn more about them and invest in the relationship, so that I can understand their business and enhance our service. I will tour the facility, and meet their people at all levels, but I will not market to them in any way. Instead I will learn about their goals, personnel, products, and operations.

- ☐ **Attend Trade Conference.** This year, I will offer to go with the client to his/her trade association conference at no charge, to learn more about his/her business and industry.

- ☐ **Read Industry Periodicals.** Within two weeks, I will view online and/or subscribe to (and read) the client's and competitor's trade journal(s) or blogs, to learn more about his/her business, industry, and jargon. The client would be delighted to learn of my interest and inform me of the best publications to read.

- ☐ **Write Industry Article.** This year, I will co-author an article or blog post with a client.

- ☐ **Make Conference Speech.** This year, I will arrange to speak at the association's next conference on a topic of particular relevance to this industry, co-presenting with a client if possible.

- ☐ **Attend Client Meetings.** This month and every two months thereafter, I will offer to attend the client's internal meetings, at no charge, to learn more about them, and offer advice on accomplishing its goals.

- ☐ **Entertain Client.** Every two months, I will entertain this client for a meal, event, etc.

- ☐ **Present In-House Seminar.** I will offer to conduct a free seminar on a useful topic.

- ☐ **Add to Mailing List.** I will ensure that this client and its key personnel are on our list.

B. New Client Development

Although it is a less-efficient way of bringing in new business, developing new clients is still important. List below one non-client target you will seek to develop business from during the coming year, and any additional support that you need to help you accomplish this.

Prospect's Name:

- ❏ I will conduct current company research.
- ❏ I will seek to visit the prospect's premises within six weeks.
- ❏ I will attend the prospect's industry/trade association meeting this year.
- ❏ I will view online and/or subscribe to (and read) the prospect's relevant trade journals and blogs within two weeks.
- ❏ I will co-author with a prospect a short, industry-focused article this year.
- ❏ I will seek to co-present with a prospect an industry association speech this year.
- ❏ I will volunteer every two months to attend the prospect's internal meetings.
- ❏ I will entertain this prospect every two months.
- ❏ I will seek to present an in-house seminar to this prospect.
- ❏ I will add this prospect to the mailing list.

III. Additional Resources

What would help you succeed with your marketing? List the top 5 in order.

(1 is "least important" and 5 is "most important").

_____ Training in how to network or work a room better

_____ Training in how to focus my marketing to achieve better results

_____ Training in how to be more effective in new-business proposals and competitions

_____ Training in advanced client-service strategies

_____ More individual instruction/coaching

_____ Assistance from colleagues (describe:)

_____ Institutional support and leadership

_____ More knowledge of firm capabilities

_____ More time

Describe:

_____

_____

_____

_____

_____

_____

_____

The Ultimate Law Firm Associate's Working-from-Home Marketing Checklist

INDIVIDUAL MARKETING PLAN: SHORT VERSION

MY 100-DAY INDIVIDUAL MARKETING PLAN

Clients: In the next 100 days, I will focus on increasing our involvement with the following existing clients (list clients and indicate the type of contact you will make with each client):

1. _____

2. _____

3. _____

Prospects: In the next 100 days, I will initiate contact with the following organizations who are not currently clients of the Firm (list prospects and indicate the type of contact you will make):

1. _____

2. _____

3. _____

Addendum

Meetings: I anticipate having the following new-business meetings (face-to-face meetings with potential buyers) during the next 100 days (list):

Current Clients	**Prospects**

Positioning: In the next 100 days, I will conduct the following "positioning/broadcasting" business-development activities (speeches, articles, seminars, mailings—general passive marketing activities):

1. _____

2. _____

3. _____

Proposals: I anticipate developing the following proposals for our services during the next 100 days (list):

1. _____

2. _____

Other: I will conduct the following "other" business development activities during the next 100 days:

Hours: I plan on devoting _____ hours per week to business development during the next 100 days.

Evaluation: The ways I will evaluate my business development efforts at the end of the 100 days will include: _____

HOW TO WRITE FOR THE INTERNET AND ENHANCE YOUR SEO

Biographies, LinkedIn pages, blog posts, and other online material can and should be used to elevate your rankings on search engines like Google (called Search-Engine Optimization, or SEO). We know roughly what Google's algorithms are looking for, which makes it possible to draft your materials in a way that uses this information to improve your results. Although there are no guarantees and the rules continue to change, leveraging this information and staying current on the trends and updates improves your chance of being found by your target audience of buyers and referral sources.

Fundamentally, Google tries to connect each search with the specific pages on credible websites that seem to best match that search. Therefore, when drafting the pages you would like ranked highly by Google, write from the perspective of a prospect seeking that information, working backwards from the specific Google searches they would conduct. Consider the exact terms they would use in the search box and use that same language in your online materials, like websites, LinkedIn, and other social media.

These days, sophisticated users are conducting longer, more complex searches, including narrow specialty areas or identifying particular types of contracts, clauses, phrases, or statutes. They include the name of the city, state, or province which means you should also if you want to persuade Google that your page is highly relevant.

Here is one of the least-known, but most-important pieces of information in this area: There are no "actual" Google search results—results differ on every computer. Google basically knows who and where you are, and tries to tailor the results to be most helpful to what you're probably looking for. This means that your search results will be very different from someone conducting the exact same search down the hall or in a different city or country. It's why when you search for "Plumber" you'll see plumbers in your local geographic area and not from Paris or São Paulo.

This reality can lead to biased results and a false confidence in your success. When you conduct a general "organic" search, your firm may receive a high ranking because Google knows your personal search history and your previous interest in that firm. But a more objective or disinterested searcher, like a prospect searching from a different city, might not find you on Google at all.

It's not unreasonable for sophisticated purchasers of legal services in the US to look for a skilled law firm in a far-flung jurisdiction by searching online. They might not do that for a major practice area in a major US city (e.g. "Boston litigation") where they can easily find a direct, in-person referral. But when seeking a professional in a smaller or less-well-known jurisdiction, Google searches become a useful option. But a firm buried on page 3 or lower will be out of competition. And that's a missed opportunity.

WRITING AN SEO-ENHANCED PRACTICE-AREA PAGE

- Describe the type of issues, services, questions, and tasks you deal with everyday.
- Engage your target audience by writing your text from your prospect's perspective. Let's consider an Intellectual Property group:
  - The firm may proudly offer a "full-service IP practice," but hot prospects rarely search for the terms "IP" or "intellectual property."
  - They more commonly seek "trade secret policy" or "registration of trade marks" or "licensing agreement." Therefore, those are the terms you should use in your practice pages as well.
- Refer to relevant statutes, landmark cases, seminal doctrine.
- Drop in the name of your firm instead of simply referring to "we."
- Include specific geography—the cities, states, provinces, and countries you serve.
- Mention that *"[Name of your firm] represents clients in the following counties:"*
  - List the counties or judicial subdivisions by name. Be careful, if the list is too long, Google may think that you're trying to inappropriately "pack" these terms, and penalize you.
- List the articles that you have written.
- If you are writing for your practice group, add: "Contact [name of attorney] at [phone number] or [email address] for more information regarding our [practice group] Law practice."
- List the names of the attorneys in the practice group, and link each name to their respective profiles.
- Add examples of work you may have done that validates the answer, e.g. client names, attorney names, cases won, and relevant statues.
- When referring to cases or statutes, you may add the complete title or link directly to them.

WRITING AN EFFECTIVE INDUSTRY-GROUP PAGE

Industry pages offer the opportunity to mix keywords that are difficult to impart in the text relating to your professional profile or practice area. This includes geographic terms (e.g. Detroit, Motor City, Michigan, Midwest), techno-legal terms (such as "molder's liens"), and statutory references (statutes, agencies, cases, and conferences).

Here is an example of a strong industry page prepared by a Detroit-based client:

> **CONTRACT AND SUPPLY CHAIN COUNSELING PAGE**
> With our roots in the Motor City and decades of combined experience, our contract and supply chain-counseling team at [Firm Name] understands the risks, costs, and challenges of the automotive and manufacturing supply chains. This in-depth knowledge enables us to provide some of the world's largest manufacturing clients with practical and detailed advice regarding how to understand, mitigate, and allocate the risks associated with selling complex automotive and non-automotive components, assemblies, and systems in a relentlessly competitive environment.
>
> We help our clients with:
> - Supply chain contracts and long-term agreements
> - Terms and conditions of purchase and sale
> - Pricing and material economics contracting, planning, and training
> - Tooling and molder's liens and asset protection
> - Supply chain risk/allocation gap analyses
> - Warranty and warranty share agreements
> - Intellectual property and trade secret agreements regarding manufacturing assets and know-how

Our team also helps automotive manufacturing companies understand and comply with the applicable safety and regulatory rules and regulations affecting their products, including:

- National Highway Traffic Safety Administration (NHTSA) rules, compliance and reporting
- Understanding and managing voluntary and mandatory recalls
- TREAD Act and Early-Warning Reporting planning and compliance
- Training, planning, and counseling for automotive manufacturers new to the United States

You will notice that any of the topics on this page could be live links that open to new pages that would speak to such topics in greater detail—you can start developing those pages when you have time.

Finally, one last word on the makeup of this page: you can also link certain of the items to other parts of the site. For instance, "TREAD Act" could link back to (i) a specific practice page; (ii) the profile of one of the attorneys who specializes on the application of this statute; or (iii) an event, conference, or article that speaks to this subject. These "lateral links" can create significant improvement both from an SEO and user-experience perspective.

Similarly, when drafting your profile, consider the references and links that can be made to specific industries.

WRITING A GREAT WEBSITE BIOGRAPHY/PROFILE PAGE

One of your most important marketing tools is a persuasive website biography. Most prospects will check out your bio before deciding whether to meet with or hire you. Website visitors are looking to identify an attorney with specific skills and experience, and match that against their particular needs.

Profile

While there are several ways to organize the content on a biography page, we suggest that you present the information as follows:

A. High-level summary

In 50 to 100 words, summarize your key skills. Refer to your position in the firm, reputation in legal circles, and standing in an industry. This is also where you can reinforce the main attributes of your firm's brand messaging with a personal message.

This short paragraph can also serve as your signature abstract that you would use whenever there is a reference to you outside the website (in a program where you are speaking, an article you wrote, a video where you are featured, etc.)

You may also list your most recent article, blog post, conference, or presentation—only one such entry is necessary here.

B. Career Highlights

In bullet-point form, list your top five highlights: this is where you are "packaging" yourself in terms that are relevant to your target clients and prospects. Where appropriate, link back to specific practice-area or industry pages on the site. In addition to your general experience, be sure to detail any particular expertise you have in the narrow specialties, niches, or industries you have selected as your marketing targets.

The career highlights should also be replicated in your LinkedIn profile.

This is also where you refer to your practice area(s), and responsibilities in such practice areas.

C. Particulars
- Education
- Publications: list articles, presentations, blogs, videos (with full title) and if possible an abstract of the subject dealt with in such material. All such material should be linked to the full version of the publication. Add a statement that you would be happy to send copies of the articles.
- Bar / Court Admittance
- Memberships
- Awards / Honors
- Social Platforms: addresses and links
- Community involvement with links to landing pages on the site for any association where you hold a leadership position. This is where you have a chance to articulate your commitment to such cause.

D. Complete resume
You can offer your visitor the opportunity to review or access a comprehensive listing of your resume. In such a listing, you should provide full descriptions of relevant matters, such as the complete name of tribunals where cases are heard, cited cases, deals, and press clippings.

Photo
Your headshot/photo should be recent and produced by a professional photographer.

Coordinates
The following basic information should also be made available:
- Name
- Office phone
- Cell phone
- Address (if multiple offices)
- vCard
- Name of assistant
- Practice area(s)
- Email
- LinkedIn profile link

DRAFTING A PERSUASIVE LINKEDIN PROFILE

This memorandum will serve as a checklist of essential items that should appear on your LinkedIn profile.

1. **List Your Full Name**
   Do not use abbreviations. Married women who changed their name should include their maiden name as well.

2. **Display a Professional Photo**
   There are reasons why some people don't want to display their photos, but this is a social networking platform. Not displaying your photo raises more questions than provides answers. Ensure that it is a professional, high-quality photograph. LinkedIn is not Facebook; do not use cropped group, vacation, or wedding photos. No props or artistic effects. Express your personality but err on the side being more conservative. Below are three LinkedIn photos with different styles. Iris Jones is outside with natural lighting, Sheenika Gandhi is inside in an office space, and Samantha Ruben is in front of a traditional solid-colored background. Each photograph conveys a slightly different impression; choose your photo's style to support the image you are trying to create.

3. **Have a Professional Headline That Properly Brands You**
   In the space underneath your name is your "Professional" or Profile Headline. It will appear in search results next to your

name, as well as next to any questions you ask or answer. It is, in essence, your elevator pitch in a few words. Do not simply put your title and firm name here: this is the place to interest anyone who finds you in a LinkedIn search result to learn more about you.

Think more in terms of "Raleigh Property Tax Attorney" or "North Carolina Family Law," rather than "Associate, Smith & Jones LLC."

4. Have Something Relevant and Timely in Your Status Update

The Status Update is about showing that you are still relevant in doing whatever you are doing. Going to an event? Share it. Attending a conference? Share it. Read something interesting that is relevant to your brand? Share it. Use your Status Update to show your relevance, and try to aim for a once-a-week update. You don't want someone visiting your profile and see a Status Update that is months old...

For those who enjoy writing, LinkedIn is an ideal platform to push out your articles.

5. Display Enough Work Experience... with Details

Your LinkedIn profile doesn't need to be a resume. One simple sentence summarizing what you did is enough to ensure that a potential reader understand the role that you had. Job descriptions provide you the perfect opportunity to pepper your profile with narrow, search engine-friendly keywords that will help you get found. For example:

> Amber concentrates her practice in the area of litigation, with a primary emphasis on litigating large commercial disputes. She regularly represents financial institutions, corporations, limited liability companies and individuals in contract, corporate, shareholder, U.C.C. and fiduciary disputes in all of the federal and state courts of North Carolina, including the North Carolina Business Court.

6. List Your Education

Put education details on your profile. What did you achieve at a certain school? Honors, awards, or activities? Mention them.

7. Get Some Recommendations

The LinkedIn "profile completeness" algorithm requires that you receive three recommendations in order to get to 100%. This is not critical, but is useful. Do not be embarrassed to ask friends who know you well to recommend you; it's a well-understood part of social networking today. And when you've done something particularly great for a client, that's the optimal time to sheepishly tell them that "the firm's marketer insisted that we ask for some LinkedIn recommendation." That is, blame "Marketing" if it'll make you feel less awkward to ask; your client will understand. Email them the link, to make it easier for them. And of course, it's only polite to recommend them back!

8. Acquire Connections

If you're on LinkedIn you should be networking. Connections are also important to help get found in the huge LinkedIn database. Rule of thumb? Multiply your age by 10 and that is the *minimum* number of connections that you should have. Join some relevant practice and industry groups and connect with the members you know. Start with your firm, any previous firms you've worked for or jobs you've held, and your law school class. Connect, connect, connect.

9. Your Professional Summary is *Essential*

The Professional Summary section is the first thing people will read, right after your headline. Don't just dump the first 2,000 characters of your standard resume into your LinkedIn Summary. This is how you will introduce yourself to your professional contacts, and future clients, referral sources, and employers. This is the most-important professional social-networking platform, so why not spend a few minutes introducing yourself? This is the place for you to tell your own story, in your own voice, typically with a bit more personality than your firm's website bio.

Addendum

Devote the time necessary to make your Summary truly great. Admittedly it can be difficult to write this way about yourself, so get some help if necessary from a professional writer, or perhaps an old friend who aced that college creative writing class.

Here's a LinkedIn profile that I wrote for my friend Joe Fasi, one of the nation's top trial lawyers. Joe's a kind, modest guy, and he wins complex ten-figure cases because juries like and trust him. It's just 333 words long, but see if it helps you start forming a generally positive impression of him and his technical skills:

> Most people know the movie "The Maltese Falcon." I am not the Maltese Falcon, but I am from the island of Malta and speak fluent Maltese. I also like to speak to jurors, and do so often and in cases with large damages at stake. I've tried over 100 jury trials to verdict, defending complex cases with enormous exposure against sympathetic plaintiffs.
>
> I haven't counted up my precise win-loss record, but a client recently asked me "how the heck I keep winning all these cases." I wasn't exactly sure how to respond to that, but I smiled and thanked him for what he intended as a compliment. Thinking about it later, I suspect the answer might partly be that I don't get involved in the games that many litigators like to play. I don't play puerile hide-the-ball tricks. I'm aggressive, but honest and reasonable. I want a fair and just resolution and, if a plaintiff wants my client to pay a lot of money, they better prove that they're darn well entitled to every penny of it.
>
> In post-trial research, juries have universally said that they liked me—they felt I approached the trial with decency and integrity, and trusted me to help them get at the truth. This is particularly important because it means I become the face of the faceless corporation. I've helped level the playing field.
>
> Fewer and fewer large cases actually go to trial. When they do, I defend them, nationwide, for companies that are among

The Ultimate Law Firm Associate's Working-from-Home Marketing Checklist

the most skilled and strategic purchasers of legal services, including manufacturers, pharmaceutical, and tobacco.

I typically handle cases as the lead trial attorney, getting hired at the outset to resolve a problematic dispute or lawsuit. Some companies use me as a their "go-to attorney," parachuting me in on the courthouse steps, either to support an existing trial team, or simply take over and handle the trial, especially the large or challenging cases.

Specialties: Product Liability, defense of nursing homes, and professional/medical liability.

11. Claim Your Personal URL

When you sign up to LinkedIn you are provided a complex "Public URL." You can customize and simplify this when you edit your profile with a couple simple steps. If you have a common name, make sure you claim your URL before others do! My LinkedIn URL is *https://www.linkedin.com/in/rossfishman/*. It's simple, and yours should be too. You can then include your abbreviated LinkedIn link on your email signature, business card, and everywhere else you go online. A quick Google search will find short videos detailing the simple steps.

12. Add Your Website(s).

You can add up to three website links. You will want to link to your blog and you may want to link to a page of any attorney directory where you're positively referenced. You should make a title for each website link — instead of having your firm name as the title, use something like "North Carolina Personal Property Tax Advisor."

13. Join Relevant Groups

You should join Groups that are relevant to your areas of interest and expertise, get active in the discussions to help meet people in your growing professional network, build your brand as a helpful and knowledgeable member of the community, and start connecting with the members as mentioned above.

HOW TO WRITE PERSUASIVE CASE STUDIES

Among the most persuasive components of a lawyer's written marketing arsenal is a current collection of case studies (also called "war stories"). Clients regularly comment that direct, relevant experience can be the decisive factor when selecting their attorneys for a particular case or matter. It is important to your marketing efforts to draft and maintain an updated collection of these examples as you go throughout your career.

In determining whom to hire, prospects are thinking, "Don't tell me that you *can* do something, show me that you've already *done* it successfully." This information is important to have in your online biographies, and for use in competitive new-business materials.

Attached is a simple, fill-in-the-blanks form to expedite the collection of this data. Before creating your own process, remember to leverage the professional staff at your firm to find out if there is additional information that you should collect or if there is firm-wide experience-management or knowledge-management system or process in place. You may choose to either fill in the blanks and start from there, or simply dictate the information following the Sample Summary format in the example shown below. With a little practice, you can dictate new case studies in just a minute or two.

LITIGATION CASE SUMMARY FORM

Case Facts:

1. The simple case caption was: _____
   _____

2. Client name: _____
   ❏ Plaintiff   ❏ Defendant

3. The court/jurisdiction was: _____
   _____

4. The *total* amount at issue was: $ _____

5. Client description - revenues, industry, etc. [e.g. $250 million pharmaceutical co.]: _____

6. Relevant issues/allegations of complaint:
   [e.g. fraud, RICO, breach of contract]: _____
   _____

7. The names of the firm's legal team: _____
   _____

8. Full description of outcome (settlement, dismissal, jury verdict etc.): _____
   _____

Case Highlights:

9. IMPORTANT: Describe how the client benefited specifically by your work (e.g. how did you save them time or money, develop an innovative strategy or tactic, etc. that another lawyer might not have considered):

_____
_____
_____
_____
_____

Sample Litigation Summary

This is a short, easy-to-read format that provides all the necessary "who, what, where, when, why, and how" information for your prospects. Remember to use plain English and short sentences, simplifying it as much as possible, targeting an eighth-grade reading level. It's not that your targets can't comprehend big words and complex sentences, just that when reading text online, they prefer not to.

Par-D, Inc. vs. U.R. Safe Company

We defended U.R. Safe, a middle-market manufacturer of smoke detectors, in a $5 million product liability, fraud, and wrongful death action in Vermont state court. The plaintiff alleged that a defective smoke detector manufactured by our client caused the fire which destroyed the plaintiff's liquor store. Following a month-long trial the jury returned a verdict in our client's favor on all counts in just 45 minutes. The case was settled on appeal, setting an important precedent in the field of liquor store conflagrations.

The Ultimate Law Firm Associate's Working-from-Home Marketing Checklist

TRANSACTIONAL CASE SUMMARY FORM

Deal Facts:

1. Client name: _____

2. Other parties involved: _____

3. The *type* of transaction was: _____

4. The *total* amount of the deal was: $ _____

5. Client description - revenues, industry, etc.
   [*e.g.* $250 million pharmaceutical co.]: _____

6. The names of your legal team:

7. Description of the deal:

Deal Highlights:

9. IMPORTANT: Describe how the client benefited specifically by use of our firm (e.g. how did we save them time or money, develop an innovative structure, *etc.* that another firm might not have done):

_____

_____

_____

_____

10. May we use the name of this client in our marketing materials?
❏ Yes   ❏ No

Sample Deal Summary

This is a short, easy-to-read format that provides all the necessary "who, what, where, when, why, and how" information for your prospects. Remember to use plain English and short sentences, simplifying it as much as possible, targeting an eighth-grade reading level. It's not that your targets can't comprehend big words and complex sentences, just that when reading text online, they prefer not to.

Acme Incorporated

We represented Acme, a $500 million mail-order company engaged in the manufacture of roadrunner-catching devices, in a coordinated series of sophisticated financings totaling $250 million. These include its public offering of $135 million of senior subordinated notes and $115 million of senior secured discount notes. Proceeds from the note offering and the term loans, along with proceeds from a prior private placement of common stock, will be used to design and construct a new jet-propulsion backpack to be marketed to desert coyotes.

NOTES

NOTES

NOTES

Need more copies of this book?

Order additional copies of this book
(in print, eBook, or Kindle format)
by emailing Ross at
ross@fishmanmarketing.com.

Contact Ross to book him for your associate-training program, firm or partner retreat, or marketing-training or Ethics/CLE programs (in-person or online).